MEMOIRS
OF AN
MI6 AGENT

Memoirs of an MI6 Agent

David Nott

Previously Published

Angels Four, *Prentice-Hall, New York, 1972*
Into the Lost World, *1975*
(Japanese title), Kasawa Bunko, *Tokyo, 1976*
Descenso al Mundo Perdido, *Monte Avila, Caracas, 1976*
The Eye of the Gods, *(novel under pen name Richard Owen) Dutton, 1978*
(Paperback version), Signet, New York, 1979
Nightmare, *St Martin's Press, 1979*
La Grenouille Qui Tue, *Gallimard, Paris, 1980*
Costa Verde, *Mondadori, Rome 1981*
Sarisariñama, *Ventura, Caracas, 1994*

Dedication

To my far off, rarely seen but dearly loved family and those closer and caring. We have all had our share of the tricks of fate. But we keep going.

Chapter 1

Recruitment

I was recruited for the British Secret Service over lunch in White's, in St. James's Street, one of London's lordliest clubs, which was founded in 1693. I made a performance of getting there on time, dead on time, pacing up the other side of the street and crossing over to the steps of the splendid house with seconds to spare, although at this stage I had no idea what I was getting into.

The porter, ex-service, probably Royal Navy, polite but with an 'I've-seen-'em-all-before' lift to his eyebrows, and the spitting image of Alf, a porter at my Cambridge college ten years earlier, asked my name. I glanced round. Satiny white paint, brand new blue carpeting. Just refurbished. But already my contact was approaching across the lobby. He was a gentlemanly, worldly man, not in the service but trusted by it as a go-between. I was to meet only one more like him in my thirty-one years as a field agent and guessed they were a rare breed and even more rarely called in. We had met, apparently casually, at an Anglo-Spanish affair in some annex somewhere several months before. I was to examine that meeting for years after. It seemed casual. But was it? Was I in fact targeted? When and how? I never got an answer and from the first days of training I knew never to ask. Now, after another gap of months, there was this luncheon, as the contact called it. During those months, I surmised, I had been screened from birth. All those worms under the stones and they still wanted to see me?

But right now in the lobby I wasn't in yet, I didn't even know what it was about.

With the contact was a tall, extraordinarily urbane but hard-headed specimen of about forty-five, the host, who led us downstairs to a booth in a cellar restaurant and suggested roast pheasant with Black Velvet (champagne and Guinness) which came in pint-size silver tankards. Making easy small talk he said that a week before at his family's country house he had gone to the ice-house for a brace of pheasant. Ice-house?

Down in the garden somewhere, deep in the earth. He'd brought them to the house and checked the date tag: 1927. The situation seemed not unknown to the contact. I, inured by years of such social imponderables, made my barely noticeable, 'well-I-never', shake of the head.

Then, civilities over, the host laid it out. He was MI6. If taken on, I would operate in South America and the

Caribbean. As a sub-editor on the *Daily Mirror* I had enough Fleet Street background to know how to use it as cover. Paralysed, I fought to take it in and to keep my face still. A million dollars, a Nefertiti nude, a moon shot, nothing could bring this exultant starburst thrill. The two men watched me as deadpan as myself.

"Sounds good," I said, with the ghost of a grin, praying I'd done it right.

The contact left after coffee. The host suggested we move to the *Ritz* for a brandy. I floated the few blocks to get there. The bar was empty. Brandies were brought. The MI6 man started to talk pay and expenses. Heart in mouth, I held up my hand.

"You mean I'm on?" I said.

"You're on." The MI6 man, amused and watchful, waited for my response.

"I'd better have another brandy," I said, forcefully killing an urge to sprint along the table tops yelling. Even so, I couldn't sit still. I stood up in my tight-cut charcoal grey suit, far too dapper for White's, I knew, took a couple of paces and sat down again. How this piece of tomfoolery had gone over I couldn't tell.

I was told to take a month to wind up my job and so on. One month from the day to take a specific train to the south coast, get off at a small station inland which I won't name because the nearby training site may still be in use. I'd be met by a driver who would ask if I was Mr. Dawson. My reply: 'Good morning. Yes, I'm Dawson'. I would then then follow what he said.

Chapter 2

Fatherhood

"You can scream all you want but all you'll get at the end is a little bastard."

It was a grim nursing sister scolding a patient in labour, in the maternity room of the Workhouse in Rice Lane, Walton Park, Liverpool. The date: 11 October, 1928. The patient was my unmarried mother. The little bastard was me.

My mother had been thrown out by her father when she became visibly pregnant. The Workhouse was her last resort. She got out of it as soon as she could walk. She found a room, put me in the bottom drawer of the dresser with a bottle and got a job as a waitress. The jobs didn't last long because she took off several times a day to see how I was. Things improved when she found the landlady heard nothing, accepted that I was not a crier and offered to look in every so often to change the bottle.

Psychiatrists might surmise that my contentment staring at the ceiling from the security of the drawer would account for later tranquillity while lolling in a hammock under Caribbean skies with a cold beer. They might also have picked up that I took equally genially to my bunk, the same shape as the drawer, on my thirty-one-foot sloop, Lady Milly, in which I crossed the Atlantic, went through the Panama Canal and up the Pacific to berth in Acapulco. Cosy minutes spent staring up at the bulkhead whether in a gale or a friendly Force 4. But they wouldn't say any such thing. They'd package it in a black cloud of post-trauma depression.

The sociologists might write a paper on how a foundling in mid-20th century Britain could jump up from such a cracked springboard to get a commission in a respected light infantry regiment and then go on to Cambridge. They'd talk about equality of opportunity and how it doesn't really count because it's not spread out enough. I'll pass on that one.

At the end of the year there was temporary shelter at home when my mother's parents took ship. It was their habit to 'winter in Gibraltar'. The sociologists could have another go here. How come my grandfather in starched collar and cane and grandma in long skirts, feathered hat and parasol could flaunter around on The Rock looking at the famed monkeys while their lovely daughter was slogging it out in a cafeteria? Because it was 1928 and her parents were old school and untouched by the whoopee of that decade. So what did they represent? It was respectability, the unforgiving church, social rigidity.

Home was a small terrace house full of treasure. Lances, war clubs, carved paddles, a long old rifle, and sawfish blades hung in the hallway. The front room, hardly used, was filled with rosewood and mahogany, porcelain, carved ivory and a grandfather clock. The living room had an authentic, old Welsh dresser, not a nail or screw in it. In a drawer I found my grandfather's card. It said he was a 'Publisher'. All he told me with great good humour, and with his pipe and brocaded, tasselled smoking cap, was that with the Cheshire Regiment in Burma in the 1880's campaigning against the 'Dakoit bandits', they'd camped and built a stockade on a slope. He was sitting in the door of his tent when a head rolled past him going downwards. He looked up to see a headless sentry keeling over. A Dakoit had leaned over the stockade and sliced through his neck with one cut.

"This head, you know, on its way down, was *bouncing.*" There was wheezy, almost soundless, asthmatic laughter as his eyes closed, looking back.

In later years I learned where to place him. There was the British colonel with long service on the North West Frontier of India and forays into Afghanistan. He said, "These fellows go out hunting game for days on end. Good shots, too. They can put a bullet in your eye at a thousand yards. Dashed sporting chaps." There was a frail old boy, a fighter pilot from World War 1. "You'd make your way back to base and see who got there and who didn't. Oh, it was great fun."

There was my company commander, DSO and MC, in Somaliland, a powerful, old-fashioned figure with a Roman nose, bald on top with flowing yellow hair behind, longer than any soldier would dare. His exploits in World War II had earned him the rank of brigadier but he had returned after the fighting to his substantive rank of major. He was a charming, gentlemanly tough who lit up when the talk was of 'doing battle'. He rarely mentioned the war but told us once of how after a desert action he had buried a fellow officer with his face shot away, in the sand. The man turned up later in Cairo. "What do you think you're doing here?" my C.O. asked. "I buried you in the desert with no face."

"Wrong chap."

"Must say, you looked a lot better then."

There was the same almost silent laugh, eyes closing. Looking back. Where are these blithe warriors now? They are still out there. But now they are called peacekeepers.

I never discovered how my grandfather ended up in this tiny place with its bow-window and two-foot privet hedge in front and a back yard loomed over by the next row of houses.

From this back yard I once saw a gigantic airship cruise slowly across the sky. I viewed it with the same awe as a German V1 flying bomb roaring in over a quiet residential area of west London, shutting its motor and diving into the houses with a tremendous bang. It fell too distant to be dangerous and I watched it with other passers-by standing quite still in the middle of a leafy street. Both events are mental films I can switch on at any time all these years later.

Back in her room my mother kept it up for a year or two and then took the marriage offer of a sailor who would take me and give me his name. Not love but need. He was a small muscular man, fastidiously clean and proper, who was on the Australia run and away most of the time. I have no memories of problems in these early years but they were lean times. Once he came back from this long run and beaming, produced his gift. It was a seven pound tin of Aussie honey.

Then came the Great Depression and the end of my childhood peace. The process started when I was about four but I was about six when I finally realized it was over. By then jobs on ships were zero. My stepfather, who I then believed was my natural father, had been a sergeant in the East Lancs. Regiment and in the trenches, literally for years. He was instilled with the respectability of a man working and earning and keeping his family, and was reduced for seven years to the shame of the dole. On his last try for a ship when I was five or six he took me urgently down to the docks. I was awed by the immense warehouses with their blind windows. He told me to sit on his bag and guard it. He ran down a dockside to where a ship was berthed. He couldn't take the bag, I worked out years later, because the bosun would have told him to bugger off for being presumptuous.

I sat for a long time. It rained. A huge man with a flat cap, big rough overcoat, and a swollen strawberry nose snatched me off the pavement, bag and all and carried me under a ledge in the warehouse wall.

"It's daft to sit in the rain, lad," he said, in a deep growl. He asked me where my dad was and I told him. He paused a moment. "Oh, aye," he said, and walked off.

My stepfather came back and to save the tram fare we walked miles back home, neither of us speaking. I never found out what he would have done with me had there been a job and he had come back for his bag and gone to the ship.

Later, my mother had to go to live in other cities to work in dismal hospital jobs to help supplement the dole and he was left with feeding, dressing and bringing up three boys. As a result, he was ground into some morose, bitter, violent other persona. Laughing in the house was forbidden. There were explosive blows to the side of the head for no apparent reason and without warning. There were thrashings with a belt when I'd cower in a corner and get hit all over my body and head. And I got soap rubbed into my eyes, up my nose and into my mouth for repeating the word 'twat' that I'd heard in the street. I didn't know what it meant.

Friday bath night we had to put our heads back to get our hair rinsed. The soapy water ran into our noses. I'd jerk forward and couldn't help calling for mummy. That earned my head being banged all around the bathtub and held down in the water until I was lifted and thrown to the floor. I have a clear memory of my brothers, aged around five and three years old, watching, fingers in their mouths, eyes wide, whom I glimpsed as I fell past them.

After the bath, our nails and toenails were clipped down to the quick. A flinch or a whimper brought a stinging slap to the face. That was the target. John, five, with a bruise on his cheek where you could see the shape of fingers was told before leaving for school, 'Just tell them you've been a bad boy'.

Another scare day was Monday when we wrote our duty letters to mother. I had to stand at the table facing a tall window which looked onto the side of a house with a tree in its back yard. I had to tear the pages off the writing pad, one each. I could not do it without ripping them. He would stand behind me and hit the side of my head. Because it hit the ear too, it sounded like a great clang and dizzied me. "Again," he'd shout and I'd rip another one and get another bang on the other side of the head. Once or twice more and the light would go hazy and the window would begin to lose shape and I'd put both hands on the table for support. He'd push me aside and I'd stagger away. Then he'd tear off the pages and hand them out. My brothers had to watch this without movement or whimper.

Mother, on her short, tearful visits bringing her pitiable pay, would plead, "Don't hit them in the face. Please, not the face." She said we were like three pale little ghosts in the back yard when she arrived.

There was no break from pressure. I went into school

in a mackintosh he had sewn up. A boy seized me by the arm to swing me round in good fun. I heard the rip in the sleeve and went to the wall and wept in despair.

He seemed to want to shout his own despair to the winds. I was in the cub scouts. There was a trip. It cost one penny. Parents and boys went to the church hall where each cub was called by name up to the stage to pay his penny. I waited unmoving in my seat, hands under my knees, panic rising. They called my name and I went up, stood at the table and announced,

"My father says he hasn't got a penny."

There were silences, coughs, little intakes of breath and, worse, titters. The cub mistress led me to the side of the stage.

One haven was the public library where I'd go for the *Just William* books and the *Adventures of a Canadian in the Foreign Legion*. Each visit I'd skip through several books in the reading room. There were passages by lady writers about being cuddled on their fathers' laps sniffing his tweed coat and tobacco. And how they savoured it for the rest of their lives.

Something approaching that position happened some months after the declaration of war in 1939. All children were moved out of the towns in the expectation of bombing that in fact didn't happen until the next year. Transporting and lodging a whole tumultuous boys' school brought us closer to the distant and revered headmaster.

He had demonstrated and handed out gas masks before we moved. When the boys had pulled them on, many puking because of the smell of the rubber, and we all looked like insects, he broke down and wept. I thought, *What a nice man.*

Two months later, tired of the wildness that gripped me after years of suppression at home, he announced to all that I was to stay behind. I'd been caned dozens of times on the hand and could take that even though it bruised the bones. When the school was empty he called me into his room. It was silent. It had no windows. He sat in a chair, pulled me towards him, and took from his desk with his left hand what looked like a flat ivory blade two inches wide with a carved handle, all of it about fourteen inches long.

He bent me over his lap, pulled up the legs of my shorts, and smoothed down the back of my thighs. I had a sudden flashback to the books. There was the tweed and the smell of tobacco.

He transferred the blade to his right hand and hit me. It made a loud smack. It hurt worse than any thrashing I'd had. I kicked my legs and struggled to get a hand back to cover them. Then there was another crack higher up my thigh. It stung and burned worse than the tip of a leather belt in the face. I gasped and squirmed and twisted but was held down. There were two more smacks.

He let me up and I was crying, jumping up and down with the pain, shaking my hands in front of me as if they were wet. For me, tobacco and tweed came with four raw, two-inch-wide welts. And total humiliation.

When I was eleven my stepfather, now enrolled in an emergency fire control squad for air raids, and a changed man, told me he was not my father. After a moment's shock I flew into a cloud of what-if's and fantasy. I did my best to get it all from my mother but she didn't want to talk about it. Then her sister Gwen came on a visit from London. She was a tall, vivid blonde whom I watched in the coming years with wonder as she manipulated headwaiters, officials, shopkeepers, anyone, with ease. She introduced me to a world of high-spirited, careless cynicism fuelled with gin-and-tonic. She told me my father was an Australian soldier over for World War I, who stayed and studied architecture at Liverpool University. Among his designs were a church, the widely-known *The Rocket* pub, and the new wing of *Lewis's*, the city's biggest department store. He died when I was three.

He was a bit of a dandy with spats, cane and fedora. He had a honey-toned speaking voice. He was already married when he chased my mother. She had run away to friends in Halkyn in Wales to escape him but he followed her. She was walking alone in a lane when he came round a bend looking for her.

"But what was he like, Gwen?" I pleaded.

"He was a rat."

So, thrashings and the fear of them, walking the knife edge every day and later disillusions, rubbed out all vestige of the cultural icon 'Father Figure'. Afterwards, I met senior men I admired. I felt sure they were made of better stuff than I was. But the vision of cuddling on a lap, cheek scraping on rough tweed, sniffing soap and tobacco and feeling loved and secure was incomprehensible. I would shake it off like something cloying. I despised the word 'father'.

On the other hand I have been blessed with six splendid children, Dominique, Viv, Millicent, David Alfonso, Carina, and Jennifer, and I love them dearly.

There's one for the shrink.

Author, Sefton Park, Liverpool 1935

Brother Peter 5 (died 2016) & author 7, Sefton Park,
Liverpool 1935

Chapter 3

Fort

It was in my head now as I walked out of the station, inoculating me from any nerves about this first contact with The Firm. There was only one other passenger leaving. Outside was a pickup with a canvas top, its driver standing alongside. I walked forward with what I figured was aplomb. The driver took a step to intercept me.

"Mr. Dawson?"

"Good morning. Yes, I'm Dawson."

"Would you like to get aboard?" he asked, pointing to the back of the truck.

As I climbed in I heard the driver speaking again.

"Mr. Philips?"

"Good morning. Yes, I'm Philips."

"In the back then, please."

A tall, lean, dark-haired number swung over the tailboard. Saturnine, I dubbed him. But what was he, recruit? Invigilator? The man sat opposite me as the truck got under way. We stared at each other for a moment.

"Going into town?" I said, tentatively.

"Not sure where this thing's going," was the reply, said with just the right touch of half humour to clothe the message, which I knew well was: 'don't ask stupid questions'. I smiled and nodded ruefully.

Not only saturnine but very smart, I thought, even more pained now at my gaffe. The rest of the journey passed in silence, both of us staring out the back.

Inside the training centre we were met by an instructor who would be one of only two people we would see there. We were now David and Bob. He showed us to our Spartan rooms in an ex-army prefab and said he'd wait for us in the common room. When we joined him, he went through security and cover. It was low-key but repeated so insistently over the next days that it grew to be part of my thinking. Cover, cover, cover.

For years later on I didn't have any.

There was a knock on the door and a stocky, grey-haired man came in.

"Ah," the instructor said, "now you're going underground," grinning at the pun. The man was a former Navy unarmed combat and small arms expert who led us to a cellar with several angled walls of up-ended railway sleepers on each side of a central passage. At the end were a space and a facing wall full of surprises. I was handed a Browning 9mm automatic.

"You fired one of these before?" the instructor asked.

"Yes."

"Right. Here's the picture. They've got one of our fellows in here somewhere. You have to get him out. Shoot his guards. Take care you don't shoot him. Just walk forward. Shoot anything that moves."

I took a careful pace thinking hard of pistol training with the 21st SAS years before. Hold your gun low, bring it up to the target, arm stiff, both eyes open, and aim it as if it were your finger pointing. Fire twice to make sure you stop him. Never mind these TV heroes with both hands holding the gun over their heads so they have to stretch their necks to see round their arms and then obscure the target even more bringing the gun down in front of it to aim. And what if they need one hand to hold on to something, suppose they're on scaffolding or on a truck?

A pop-up plywood head bonked out of a slot on my right. I fired once, ears ringing at the noise in this confined space, and before I got the second shot off it hinged back and disappeared.

Jesus, they move things here. Got to shoot fast without snatching at the trigger.

I took a pace, glancing left and right. A bonk warned me there was a target on the right. I fired, one shot only again. The target hinged out of sight again and there was another and then another on the left. I fired at each in turn.

No way I'll get two shots at one target, I thought.

I got to the end of the walk and took a first step into a cross passage that led left and right. There was a sudden whirring on the right and a full length plywood figure came careening down a cable to whiz past in front of me. I got one shot off as it rattled on down to the left along a low, nasty passageway with a red light bulb and a figure held down by two enemy thugs. Really into the game now, I was indignant.

"Bloody sods," I muttered.

I fired once at each, high up, so as not to hit 'our fellow'.

"Right. Leave it now," the instructor said. I pointed the gun down and came back to him. The instructor took the Browning.

"How many shots?" he asked.

I went over it, trying to remember.

"Six."

"Yeah. Well. Better keep count in your head so you don't have to think."

The instructor walked forward to check the targets and paste over the holes. He came back and handed the gun to Dark and Saturnine.

"You have enough rounds in there. You've used handguns before, right?"

"Right."

I watched closely. I knew now that Saturnine had been in Popski's Private Army, one of the more extraordinary Special Forces groups operating in World War II, sweeping hundreds of miles across the North African desert in battle jeeps, navigating by astrolabe, attacking an incredulous enemy out of nowhere and vanishing into the wilderness again. Then later fighting on quite different terrain up in Italy.

I watched him move forward, alert but relaxed, then turn and fire. One shot only, I noted, feeling I was in good company. Saturnine went through the same sequence, not a movement wasted, deliberate.

We talked over the one shot two shot question that night. "You use a handgun only up close. You shouldn't miss. One 9mm slug will stop anyone but a huge man," said Saturnine.

Next day we were driven to a car park outside a pub. "Walk about a hundred yards further and you'll see the entrance to a military base. There's no guardhouse. Just walk in and walk around as if you were going somewhere, take it all in, objects and distances. Later you'll draw a map of it. I'll see you here in three hours," the instructor said.

We watched him drive away and thought it out.

"There's no sentry but what if we're asked what we're doing inside? We need a story," said Saturnine.

"We're down here on holiday and saw the entrance. Thought we'd have a look round. Maybe it's an old manor house?"

"So where are we staying? Why are we on holiday together? We work together? Where's the family? Do we have a family? Do we have a car? Why didn't we drive in if we're so sure we can just walk in?"

"It won't hold up. And if they question us apart? That'll sink us," Saturnine said.

Well, will it? I was thinking.

Chapter 4

Dynamite

We three boys scoured through the huge slate quarry. It was Sunday and the great seventy-foot high galleries were deserted. We were all thirteen years old.

"There, that's it," I said.

I was pointing at a squat, thick-walled hut on the floor of the quarry, two hundred feet below.

"That's the powder house. Dynamite. Fuse wire. If there are detonators too, we can blow anything up."

George and I knew all about it and we longed to show off to Harry on his first delinquent excursion. Months before we had searched through another huge slate quarry, this one in Bethesda. We'd found Rockrift sticks of dynamite in thick, beige, greasy paper, fuse wire and black powder in little granules we could run through our fingers. It was all old, dampish, and dumped in a wooden box in a blast shelter.

Day after day we lit fires on the moor and threw in the

dynamite then the powder. Nothing. We'd peel the paper off one end of the sticks and push the fuse wire in and light it. The spark travelled weakly along it and we'd throw ourselves behind a rock when it was about to touch. Nothing.

"It's got to be in a borehole or a crack. Not out in the open," George said.

We tried it in between rocks with more piled over it. Nothing.

"Back to the quarry," we said.

Then one day we found, embedded in a strong wooden crate full of sawdust, a thin, red, tin box. In it were lines of slim, aluminium tubes in grooves. We didn't even know what they were called. We had never heard of detonators but the care with which they were housed told us they were dangerous and a part of the chain that led to a proper explosion.

We stuffed sticks of dynamite down our shirts and filled our pockets with powder. George grabbed a coil of fuse wire and I held the detonator box in my hand. We scrambled hundreds of feet up the ladders and wagon-ways to the top of the quarry and out onto the moors.

We found an old, drystone wall. I opened the box and took out a detonator. We examined it. We could see it was empty for about two thirds of its length. The rest had to be explosive, the explosive tip. We saw too that the diameter was the same as the fuse wire. We tried to insert the end of the fuse. It went in. We looked at each other and nodded. I delicately pushed in the wire until it stopped.

How to stop it falling off? I squeezed the end of the tube with my nails and felt it give a little. Then, while all the explosive experts turned in their graves, I put the detonator into my mouth and with the explosive tip tickling my throat, felt with my teeth for the end where the fuse went in and bit down on it, clamping it tight.

George opened the end of a stick of Rockrift and passed it over. I pushed the detonator and fuse gently into the soft dynamite and closed the paper round it. He threaded it into the wall between heavy stones and tamped it in with turf. He cut the wire two feet from the charge and lit it with a match. It fizzed suddenly and we scampered twenty feet and ducked behind a boulder.

The explosion boomed over the moor, and the fragments pattered around us as we held our heads in our arms. Then we were up and running to the wall to see the smoking, blackened gap. We sniffed that marvellous smell of cordite we'd never fail to recognize again and whooped and danced about. George suddenly grabbed me.

"We've got to get out of here, now. They'll have heard that in the village and will be wondering what the hell."

The men in the single-street village across the moor would be coming out for a look. Many were quarrymen. We ran west through the gorse until we judged it time to turn north and then circle round the village and come in from the opposite direction to the quarry.

On the way George said firmly,

"We have to dump this stuff. We'll put it under a rock where we're sure we can find it again."

I hated to leave it, but he was right. We found a flat boulder with a jutting end and piled the loot underneath, sealing it with bracken. We noted its distance from a wall and put two small stones on top so we would recognize it.

"Let's just go back slowly as if we've just been out for a walk," said George.

Now, this time, we demolition men were scrabbling round the old powder house in a different but more remote quarry on the coast of Anglesey. Harry watched us, confused. We found an old, round biscuit tin with a browny-yellowy sludge in it. We felt it. George sniffed it.

"That's dynamite. It's got water in it," he said.

I opened an old sack and whooped.

"Fuse wire and, and look!" I held up a pair of detonators, grey and nicked, old stuff. We grinned at each other.

"We better not blow anything up in the quarry," said George.

"Let's just make a bang, then. In here," I said.

We pushed the detonator (now we knew the word) into the mush, uncovered. George cut the fuse and scraped the end. I pushed it into the detonator and crimped it with my teeth. I pushed it into the damp stuff in the tin and George lit the fuse. We watched it burn with more energy than we expected and scrambled for the door.

Harry was in the way and we pushed him on. We were still jammed in the door fighting to get out when the explosive blew. We popped out sprawling in a heap feeling ourselves for missing limbs. Then we were laughing and Harry was shaking us.

"What was that? How did you do it?"

Harry, with a keen brain, and later a scholar of St John's College, Cambridge, grilled us.

"It's nothing, Harry. Just a bit of dynamite," said George.

"And fuse wire."

"And a manky old detonator."

Perhaps it was the remoteness or the soft sounds of the sea from over the side of the quarry. Whatever it was, we got careless. Above us on the other side of the quarry floor were some one-floor buildings. We crossed over and looked through the windows. There were cabinets, papers, and a tea urn, and hanging on the wall were some raincoats.

"Maybe there's dynamite here."

We tried the windows. Locked. Suddenly, Harry, the class swot, serious, never in trouble, grabbed a stone and broke a pane, wild-eyed, and grinning like a demon. George and I looked askance at each other but Harry had already put his hand through and opened the catch. We pushed the window up and crawled inside, searching. In one drawer there was a cardboard box with loose coins in it and a few notes.

"I don't think we should take money. Like burglars," said George.

"But you'd take dynamite," said Harry.

"That's different. We could be on the bomb squad." It

was still World War II and the teams that deactivated unexploded bombs were heroes.

"We shouldn't hang around in here. We'd better get outside at least," I said.

We got out and pushed the window down. We stood there arguing it over, George and me facing Harry who suddenly jerked upright, his face white.

"Watchman," he whispered.

We whirled and saw part of an army greatcoat flapping at the corner of the building. In a flash, like wild deer, we were running for our lives down and across the floor of the quarry to a gap in the high walls. We reached it and peered over the edge at the sea far below. We climbed a ridge we never would have dreamed of attempting and burst out onto the moor above. We didn't stop running for miles.

Some days later, back in Liverpool, George and I got a telegram from Harry.

'Meet me tomorrow outside Adelphi ten a.m. Urgent. Police.'

We met. Harry, who'd stayed in Bangor when school closed, had had a visit from the police. How had they tracked him? Harry said the watchman had been listening to us as we wrangled over the money. He heard our accents and knew we're evacuees from Liverpool. It was easy to figure out we were in Bangor. They talked to the teachers and they knew I was still there."

"You told them you were with us?"

"We were seen, weren't we?"

He was right. We were in deep trouble. Harry, who'd

thought it all out, said we had to tell exactly the same story when interrogated apart. He'd told them our route through the quarry, step by step. And we had to repeat it exactly. He'd said, 'Yes, we'd heard a boom, and no, sir, we had not broken a window. We're not scruffs from the Dock Road, sir'. He rehearsed us in the street in front of the Adelphi, over and over again, with the story. He said we had to hope the watchman was prowling around because he heard the bang and not because he heard the window breaking. We had taken nothing from inside and disturbed nothing. Thank God, George and I agreed, that they'd got to Harry first. The school's prize pupil, he was surely supported by the teachers whereas if it had been us…

Next month, back in Bangor, the police came to the school and took me into an empty classroom. I followed the ten points we'd set for the story to the letter. George did the same. Nothing more was heard from them. But it left me cocky. I was a bomber, a hard nut under questioning, a special operations man.

Hard stuff. Great Wall, North Wales, 1973. This is for young tigers in their twenties. I was 45 and feeling it.

Pico Jahn on Pico Bolivar, 5007m, Venezuelan Andes. El Virtigo behind, first ascent with George Band of Everest team, 1962

Warming up on easy Aiguille, Chamonix, 1968

Chapter 5

Airfield

I shook my head at Saturnine, thinking of that police grilling in the empty classroom.

"It's no good. We need a story we can repeat word for word, every step of the way. We'd have to rehearse it till we've got it off pat. We'd need a day just to get our background worked out let alone what we're doing here. There isn't time."

Saturnine looked curiously at me, surprised by my vehemence. I was petrified about losing the job, of course.

"Well, we've got to go in," he said.

We walked up the road. I was thinking hard. This is what they mean by cover. This is what it feels like not to have any. Naked. If somebody stops us we might get away with it acting it out. Couple of dopey idlers with little to do. But if they get serious and question us separately we haven't a hope in hell of getting away with it.

We came to the gate and went in looking about

goofily. We walked what seemed like half a mile to the first buildings, looking around, gassing away about nothing at all. I fixed in my head the angles of the roads leading off, counting the buildings on each side. Then Saturnine said,

"Why don't we split up? I'll go down here and you go on this way. We can cover twice the ground. See you back here in two hours."

"Fair enough," I shrugged.

I walked on staring through the trees. By God, it's an airfield. There's one of those big radar planes. And three transports. DC3's. I left the road and skirted the field in the cover of the trees, listing planes and buildings.

If they find you here you're really in trouble. Have to pretend you're taking a leak. You'll be lucky if they don't shoot it off.

The airfield was the far limit of the base. The main group of buildings was back where Saturnine had gone. I went on to see what the boundary was like. Nothing. Just a hedge and a barbed wire fence. No trouble to a saboteur. I turned back to the road and took another side road parallel to Saturnine's. One, two, three sleeping quarters, can't call them barracks. There's a mess and there by God coming towards me a group of civvies and some RAF men in uniform. I made a show of looking at my watch and turned, walking back briskly with a 'dammit-I'm-late' stride. Soon I spied Saturnine, putting on the same show. We continued on heading that long half mile to the gate.

A car came up from behind and stopped. The driver offered a lift.

We got in the back.

Good way to get out of here at least.

Then we noticed the driver was a burly military police officer, a red-faced bruiser in fact.

"Day off, then?" the bruiser said.

"That's it. Lovely weather for it," chirped Saturnine.

"It's still warm for autumn," I said. "Might surprise us with a brisk winter though."

Thank God, the gate. Before the car could turn left into the road Saturnine piped up fast as ever,

"We're meeting a bloke at that pub over there."

"Yes, it's very good of you but can you drop us just here?" I said.

"Sure," said the bruiser, a touch bemused, looking round at us. We got out quick, smiling thanks, and waving goodbye. He was still looking at us through the windscreen. Then he drove off after a few seconds. It seemed like a week.

We breathed out slowly. In a few moments the instructor's car drew up and took us back to base. After lunch and a beer we drew the maps and handed them in. There was no comment at all from the instructor. I wondered how much what appeared to be a little boy-scout initiative exercise had shown him. It was the planning we *didn't* do that got me. If that had been for real we'd have been two steps from a bullet in the neck. We waited for the instructor to drive it home, to go over it but there wasn't a word said. In fact the extraordinary discretion of the Service was beginning to penetrate. They are a very subtle lot and they couldn't have arrived at so hands-off a training policy without years at it. Were they the same in actual operations? And what's more, did the instructor expect questions like this? Neither of us ventured a single query and we said not a word to each other about it. If laconic is the style then so be it.

After lunch, underground, I needed to let off steam. What I wanted was to riddle the moving target in the seconds it swung across the end of the walkway. I pictured its passing in my head and counted from when it appeared on the right... 'thousand one, thousand two' to when it vanished again down the passage on the left. Two seconds. Six shots would be a marvel. I wheedled until the Navy man said, "Alright, say when you're ready."

Saturnine was wearing a snide grin. I said, "Now," and the target swung in from the right. I fired as fast as I could moving the gun to the left without stopping. I got three rounds off. We went forward to look. One shot on the edge of the target.

"Well, I nicked him."

There was no comment.

Three days more drill on cover and security, never a peep on invisible ink, dead drops, cut-outs and so on, all that stuff in the spy books, and we came to the last test the next morning.

We carried our bags into the town ready for the

London train later and moved about independently from checkpoint to checkpoint which we'd memorized, before our last rendezvous, timed, in a large, ratty café. At the pre-set time, Saturnine said,

"I'll go first if you like? You finish your coffee."

He left and I waited to let him get clear. Suddenly he appeared in the doorway again, before threading his way fast through the tables towards the back of the café.

"Gestapo," he hissed, as he passed me.

I was up in a flash and followed him round the counter, through a swing door, into a kitchen, through the employees and out through a back door where we separated and got away.

Later we met at the station for the train to London. The instructor was there. He was laughing, explaining to me,

"Brilliant. We had a policeman stop Bob and ask to look in his bag. Bob looked down and said, 'good God, I've got the wrong bag. Just a moment'. Then he turned and scooted off to get you out of the café. Bloody marvellous."

We both had a heavy hangover from last night drinks and had little to say on the way back to London.. Here we found our way to a safe house with the address memorized: a dingy terrace house where, in a stuffy, heavily curtained room, a thick-accented eastern European gave us a run down on Communism. It was rarefied political science. I managed to make a karate chop in his direction when he was not looking. It had become our mocking signal for cloak and dagger and convulsed Saturnine. Once free we left and went to the nearest pub for a final drink. Still sick, half a beer was all we could stomach. We left the pub and stood for a moment in the street.

"Well, we won't meet again, so cheers," said Saturnine, and walked away.

Turning away myself I remembered another goodbye like that, short, sudden and final.

Chapter 6

Blitz

It was the fifth of seven straight nights' bombing. The May blitz on Liverpool, 1941.

Docks, shipyards, vessels in the river, the naval Western Approaches Command Centre; all were targets.

Bombers 680, bombs 870 tons, incendiaries 112,000, homeless 75,000, dead 1,740.

They came in quicker than usual after the sirens and we had no time to run the four blocks to a bomb shelter. In the cellar of the house we sat on the steps.

I was eleven, my mother in her thirties. The house shook with the explosions and we could hear stuff falling off the shelves in the kitchen. Then the floor moved and we knocked against the wall, deafened. It was not normal bombing. It made us jerk upright and cling. I felt the muscles of her back juddering. Mine too.

The candle guttered. Dust fell in streams from between the boards of the ceiling. They were dropping 1000lb 'landmines' by parachute, big long fat things, with a round nose and no tailfins, the last word in indiscriminate bombing. Terror bombing. It was two hundred yards away and lifted us off the steps.

I said we should run for it. She nodded. Outside there was a clear, starlit sky. The sound of bombs whumping in the distance answered by the crack of ack-ack guns, far too few to defend a city, could clearly be heard. We crossed Smithdown Road to keep close to the nine-foot walls of the hospital as cover.

Suddenly there were bombers overhead again with that peculiar double beat of the engines. We had only got a few yards when the guns opened up. There was a ping on the asphalt and then a loud clang. Shrapnel. I stooped and found a seven-inch shell splinter, an inch wide, twisted and its quarter-inch sides serrated and needle sharp. I felt faint with a vision of one of us hit and killed. Not both of us. One. There in the street. Behind us a bomb cut away the front of a three storey building and exploded in the street. Now incendiaries cracked and fizzed on the asphalt and split the slate roofs. We ran like the wind.

The shelter was a big cellar with pit-props under the ceiling. We sat on a bench close to the wall. Opposite was a ring of seats and a family with their backs to us. Behind us was a man telling a landmine story, a rough old lad with a bulky overcoat, collar up, and a flat cap on his white hair.

"Ye know 'Arry Smith? Last night when 'e was in the shelter a bloody landmine came through the roof of his 'ouse and didn't explode. He came through the back door into the kitchen and there was this bloody great bomb sitting in his rocking chair. He nearly shat on the dog."

My mother was shaking. Laughing silently. Me too. A woman leaned towards the old man, smiling affectionately. "Daft old bugger," she said.

When the next wave came over the closest bomb of the night knocked us off the bench. As the lights went out the family jumped up and ran towards us stumbling over their seats. The father's mouth was a wide 0 in his face, screaming, his arms flailing. But we heard nothing against the noise up top. We sat tight, hand in hand in the dark.

Sometime later an air raid warden came in and lit candles and a lantern. An hour later the steel door banged open and wardens led in about twenty people, dusty and dazed, and sat them on a row of benches on our right. There was an unexploded bomb two streets away. They had been evacuated and brought through the pounding night. I looked at them dully, and nudged my mother.

"There's Granddad and Granma," I said. Numbed, she did not reply. She didn't even look up.

At 3 a.m. the all-clear sounded. The raid had lasted five hours. We helped my grandparents up the steps and took them home treading on crackling glass shards from the blown-out windows and stumbling over rubble thirty yards from home where a bomb had hit a house and covered the road with debris. Over the docks a great column of black smoke rose against the yellowing sky.

The fires were still burning and would be when the bombers came the next night. Crumps and thumps sounded from the river. They had hit an ammunition ship, someone said.

Late morning I went out to see the house that had been hit on the next block. The bomb, a small one, had sheared off the front wall. The collapsed roof, ceilings and floors of the two upper stories were held up by the ceiling of the ground floor. As usual, the staircases were intact, still pinioned into the walls. That's why they told you to get under them during a raid. I went round to the back door, scrambled up and dropped into the yard. The house had been empty. I crossed to the window glancing up to see the third floor wall bulging out over where I stood. Dust and pellets of mortar were drifting down from it. Inside, the weight of debris had collapsed the ceiling to within four feet of the floor. The beams were creaking. Rivulets of dust ran down from the cracks and plaster was falling. I could feel it was about to crash but as I turned to get out I saw a movement in the shadow at the far side of the room.

It was a small dog lying on rags. "Dog," I said, "come out of there. C'mon, boy." He didn't move. "This whole bloody thing will fall any minute," I warned him. The dog stayed put. Glancing up scared at the bulging wall I pushed the window up and got inside. I ducked under the ceiling and got near him. "Dog," I whispered, "come here." Bent, I shuffled fearfully over to him and put my hand out to pick him up. He snapped at me and I saw he was missing a paw. A sharp point of bone stuck out of blood and puss.

There was a lurch from the tons of rubble over my head and I grabbed him under one arm and slowly edged to the window. *Jesus. Just a minute more*. I squirmed over the window sill, ran out of the yard and into the street. It was only thirty yards from my back door.

I heated water, and cleaned up his wound. There was no way I could touch that jutting, splintered bone so I padded it with a rag and sticky plaster. I saw that one eye was blank, cloudy white, so I called him Smokey. He looked a little better after some bread and milk and I was able to stroke him. "Poor fellow," I said, "three legs and one eye."

But soon he got fidgety and nervous, whining and hobbling to the door. "D'you want to go out?" I said. "Walk in the street?" I carried him out and set him down on the pavement. He was unsteady on his three paws so I let go him without a leash. He surely wouldn't get far. But about fifty yards from the corner he began to go faster. In the last ten yards before the crossroads I was running and shouting, "Smokey, Smokey."

He scuttled round the corner. I ran full tilt and looked along the street he'd taken. He was nowhere. I called him and searched the rubble of a bombed house on the next corner.

He'd gone. I never saw him again.

My mother, Annabella Gwynedd, 'Blitz Mom' 12 Sep 1942

Chapter 7

Six Guineas

My pay was six guineas a week. A guinea was one pound and one shilling. It was worth that when Dickens was writing and it was still worth that in 1955 on the *Liverpool Daily Post*. It is a solid provincial newspaper which took two men from Oxford each year as trainees. I was from the other place, Cambridge, but my wily letter of application got me an interview. During it the proprietor, a member of the owning Jeans family, said, a little wearily, "And I suppose you too see yourself as drama critic for the paper?"

I guessed he was up to here with all those Oxonian, dreamy-eyed English Lit. graduates. "I wouldn't know where to start," I said.

"Right. You're on. I'll take you as a third man."

I had applied to all major national newspapers and to several provincials. Most didn't reply. When they did it was to say their newsmen started at sixteen making tea for the sub-editors and we don't need any university poufs.

The training on the *Post* was the best anywhere. One year covering reporting, sub-editing news and features, editorial page and work on the stone putting your pages to bed, machine-room, photo labs. We even got to write a third editorial leader, some nights when there were a couple of inches of space. What they were looking for was good news-subs, the ones who carve the story for the space available and put a headline on it. Above all, make no mistakes.

I ended the year on the editorial page.

But because he liked my stuff as a reporter on boys' school boxing, the sports editor assigned me as boxing writer every Thursday night for professional fights. On my ringside stool I soon got blood splashed on my notebook and later waved it under the noses of gagging colleagues in the news room. But I got to travel, too. Once I went to Paris where our local middleweight, a clean, handsome fighter, got pounded by a French ex-miner in an enormous, thunderous stadium.

In the middle of all this, I boobed. One of the reporters' perks was to visit the transatlantic liners at the docks to interview any important passenger on board and then to eat from the enormous ship's menu. We used the narrow, crew's gangway and showed our press card to a bosun, usually a big tough, waiting at the top. Behind and in front were men with no pass who just said 'crew', and were waved aboard.

In 1956 my maternal uncle, splendidly named Llewellyn ap Olaf Salusbury Hughes, who lived in New York, came over on a visit. He was going back on the Cunard liner *Franconia* which was making her last voyage. Two family members were allowed on board, my mother and Aunt Gwenllian. We'd all been rollicking around in a pub. I told my brother John what I knew and he was game. We hustled up the gangplank and grunted 'crew', in a rough Liverpool accent, turned left on deck, went aft, squirreled about a bit in the passageways and eventually got to the passengers' quarters. When we got to the cabin Llew and Gwen roared their approval and passed the scotch.

When the warning went for non-passengers to disembark and a steward thumped the door shouting 'all ashore that's goin' ashore', John and I decided to stay. My mother went off shaking her head and Gwen with her, laughing. With the whiskey way down and the ship well out into the Irish Sea we went up to the bar which was jumping. We whooped it up until early morning when the ship anchored at Cobh. They finally nabbed us when we tried to sneak down to the lighter, moored alongside, to go ashore. We were hauled before the captain, with his chief mate and the burly bosun.

"With complete respect to you as captain and final authority I can only say we didn't hear the warning," I said.

Silence and the bosun's veins swelling. "Of course, we had a bottle of scotch in the cabin," I said weakly.

"You will pay the fare," said the captain.

"Sir, with due respect. We didn't hear the warning and anyway we don't have any money."

"Go and get it from your uncle, Mr Hughes."

"Can't do that, sir."

"I could put you in irons." The bosun leaned forward avidly.

"I'm truly sorry, sir, but there's nothing I can do."

The captain pushed back from his desk and glowered at me. It was his beloved, 20,000-ton sumptuous ship's last voyage and he had other things to think of besides us two little pests.

"Get them out of here. Put 'em ashore and call the police."

We went down the rickety ladder to the lighter. Llew leaned over the side grinning.

"Say hello to Ireland for me. So long, boys."

At the wharf there were no police but a couple of Irishmen came up. "Are you'se the guys that stowed away?"

"That's us."

"Well, bloody good."

We found the post office and I sent a telegram to the office. 'Stuck on *Franconia*. Now in Cobh. Trying fly back'. We walked out of town to hitch. No traffic. We found the station and there was a train to Dublin. We got the tickets and bought a can of sardines and some hardtack biscuits. We walked along the corridor looking for seats.

Compartment after compartment was full of poor children drooling and lolling in awkward positions. Then we met up with nuns and nurses in stiff uniforms patrolling the coaches. It was a hospital train. Our urgent dreams of a cold beer in the lounge car evaporated. Haggard, we walked up and down waving to the kids. All the way to Dublin. Here we found *Aer Lingus*, the Irish airline. I pulled myself together, marched in and talked like never before. My point was that we had no money but John would stay as hostage in Liverpool airport until I could go to the bank. A crowd of airline people gathered round, laughing about our escapade on the ship.

"Don't you worry, Mr. Nott. Pay in our town office there. John can go home too."

A devastating colleen hostess led us out to the plane. Back in Liverpool and on my way to the *Post* I met one of the Oxonians.

"My God. You should have heard the uproar in the office when your telegram arrived.

"Every man on the paper knows about it."

"And the boss?"

"How could he not know?"

Shortly afterwards I wanted, ungratefully, to move on and discovered I was quite dispensable when no objection came from upstairs to my shift to *Reuters* in Fleet Street. This grand old news agency worked on a whole open floor of its big building. I started on the Central Desk, the guts of the world-wide operation, and was moved to the European desk after three weeks. I could look around at some lonely subs on remote regional desks.

We sat for eight hours on hard chairs surrounded by hammering telex machines that could spout copy faster than we could tear it off, sub-edit it and throw it in the out-trays for the lads to run round and collect. There was no lull. You could never get up and stretch and wander over to the next desk to josh with someone.

On my first day I'd gone out to Earl's Court, an area of London reputed to have no inhabitant under twenty and none over twenty-eight. Mucho whoopee. I took an address from a shop window and went to see the landlord. He showed me a room in a flat. There were four more rooms and a kitchen and bathroom both filled with panties, bras and stockings hanging up to dry. I looked at them and then at him.

"Yes. Well, four girls live here," he said.

"Lovely. But what are they going to say when they find me in here?"

"You'll be all right."

I wasn't all right. This was no harem. It sounds like a young fella's dream. But they were free spirits and I was frankly in the way. After two weeks I moved upstairs.

That was the one place I shouldn't have gone to at the office. Upstairs. I was now earning seventeen pounds ten shillings a week and was itching to get abroad as a correspondent. Unfortunately a hundred others, better men than me, wanted the same but had the sense to shut up. I took a letter up to the boss. This was unprecedented. The European editor, a very old hand, called me over.

"You sent a letter to the boss? You asked for a raise? You asked to be sent abroad?"

"Yes."

"You're a bloody fool."

Seeing my career stuck in the mire, Lady Luck intervened. She was a dynamo American, Casey Herrick, daughter of a famed New York senator. She wanted to launch a weekly in Geneva for expats. Tipped off by a stringer over there I called her and telexed my CV. She told me to go over and get vetted. Now there are many fine reporters and sub-editors but few of them could do page make-up and stone work as well, thank you *Daily Post*, and fewer spoke French, which I did. Once more a high honcho who could change my life nodded and said, 'you're on'. She also said, "Start now," so I didn't give the usual month's notice to *Reuters* and told them so by cable.

Some months later the top man on Central Desk passed through and met with us local newsmen. When I uncomfortably told him who I was he laughed. "You're the one who sent a cable telling *Reuters* to go to hell," he said.

In Geneva, work for the first edition of the *Weekly Tribune* was rough. I ran round reporting, wrote all eight pages, subbed them, did make-up, and wrangled with the *Tribune De Genève* which would print it. Casey, run off her feet selling ad space, holding off creditors, gave me uppers in the morning and downers at night. It was that bad. When the first edition came out we went with her husband, who I could see had long given up stemming the typhoon he'd married, to a one-room restaurant with nothing whatever as décor but superb steak and rugged local wine. I popped no pills that night.

Later, when we got into stride, there came my Smith College princess, Day Dobbert, and skiing. In my first car, a third-hand Ford, we drove over to nearby French resorts. In one of these, Morgines, the ski-lift was stopped for heavy snowfall. About ten we saw it moving and rushed over. We were the only customers. Up top, there was deep powder which I knew nothing about. I took off downhill, skis and feet invisible under the snow and I piled up when I tried to slow. I was entangled and my right leg hurt so bad I shouted. Day, who hadn't started down waved to the only two skiers up there. A sturdy athlete, a Finn, whooshed down to me and I shouted to get my right ski off. The twisted leg was on the point of snapping. Unnerved by my howling he yanked it and the fibula broke. He stood me up, bad leg on the downside of the slope, gave his ski-sticks to Day, turned his back to me, bent his knees, put his hands under my armpits and lifted me above his head. He took off without a word and skimmed downhill.

I shut my eyes on the left hand turns because they brought my aching leg over the drop. *If he falls…* We got to less steep ground. Two rescue men were there with a sled. One behind to brake. A girl from the bar where I was up to my antics the night before skied over. I was lying on my side clutching my leg in both hands, gasping. Her face was concerned and upset. Then she recognized me with a start, turned and skied away.

"You silly man," she said, over her shoulder.

After one year or so calling myself 'editor', I thought I'd better get back to Fleet Street. I got in as a news-sub on the *Daily Mirror*, a rip-roaring tabloid with the world's top circulation of six million. It was in the old *Mirror* building in Chancery Lane, with the scruffiest editorial floor and canteen in London. But it was a formidable operation every night. The staid broadsheets and the upmarket middle class spurned it as sensationalist with screeching headlines down to mid-page and no content. But a wise old-timer on the Street wrote that more brainpower went into its production than in all the flagship papers put together. He was right. There were eight subs on the desk and three chief subs mainly on the four to midnight shift. There was easy camaraderie but a definite hierarchy. There were two young stars who were quiet most of the time and then jerked, nerves strung, into frantic work when the front-page story was handed to one of them by a chief sub at the head of the horse-shoe table. They'd have reams of reports from the news agencies, a correspondent's story, and instructions from the top of the table.

These looked like a doctor's scribble but were phenomenally complicated and precise to the last dot. There could be a 72-point headline, one line across five columns down into two, 24-point two-line sub-head, one line two columns second line one and one half columns. Text, one inch of 10-point bold, then three and a half inches 8 point. The aces would get the picture in their heads and delve into the telex reports for the gist of it all. I saw them breathing faster, throwing all they had into it.

In a shockingly short time the chief sub, tensed up himself and looking at his watch, would bark, "Can you give me a start, Bob?" Shortly after, Bob would pass the headlines. They were snatched by the chief sub, studied tight-lipped and sent up immediately to the printers. He would let his breath go and say, leaning back in his chair,

"Good one, Bob." As a test, we'd read the one or more columns of the *Times* and *Telegraph* early editions on the same story, pick out the essential points and check with the *Mirror's* three or four inches. All those points were there.

I never wrought one of these miracles. I was on a low rung of the ladder. But I was earning top rate pay of thirty-three pounds a week. Ten went in taxes, ten on rent, and the rest in Earl's Court pubs.

By coincidence, all but immediately after the White's meeting I was called in by the chief editor, Mr. Dinsdale, famed as a man-eater of errant subs. He began quietly but I could see in an instant where he was going. I interrupted saying, "May I take this chance to give a month's notice because I have another job?" He looked relieved.

"Don't worry about the notice. Collect your pay and good luck."

In the next days I was escorted by a tall, impeccable MI6 man with bowler and umbrella, into the offices of a lordly broadsheet, a leading conservative journal, and up to the penthouse to a side of journalism I'd never seen – the sumptuous offices of the real nabobs. Big and richly furnished, the office mirrored the man who stood up to greet my guide.

"Well, old chap, how *are* you getting along?" Standing to one side was a famous name in political commentators. He did not smile and carried a whiff of disapproval my antenna picked up immediately. The nabob greeted me with interest. I figured rapidly that he and bowler hat were of the old school who still saw intelligence work as the Great Game. The way it was when our chaps with dyed faces and hands and in tribal robes, snuck over the frontier of the Raj into Afghanistan to scout out what Imperial Russia was to up to and which bandit chiefs would take a bag of gold to leave the Czar and come over to the Queen.

I came out with a letter of accreditation as a stringer and an uneasy sense from the other man that this was a loaded trick. I later learned that there's nothing more hated by newsmen than an intelligence man using them as cover.

At any rate I had my dubious press pass, the last I was to have, and was ready for my first posting overseas.

Chapter 8

Arrival in Venezuela

Culture shock happens only to the over-sensitive. But when they wheeled the steps up to the door of the plane and I started down them at La Guaira airport for Caracas, December 1960, my first sight of this beautiful country was ten sloppy, slouching, sneering, leering, street-corner boys in National Guard uniforms. In a few seconds they provided an insight into Latin Americanism at its worst.

The newspapers and writers call them 'proud nations'. What they are is prickly, and keenly aware of their failure to forge viable, prosperous, governable countries. They've been there five hundred years and they still don't clear the gutters in the dry season to avoid floods when the rains come. There can be denigration of the US, covering profound envy, and attempting to cover political and economic mediocrity so glaringly underlined by contrast to the success of their northern neighbour whose people came a century later than themselves to the New World and made something of it. Individuals of all classes are in too many cases obsessed with respect from others, indignant if they don't get it, ignorant of the fact that it has to be earned. There is also the faction that believes the Latino is an effervescent charmer. Darwin noted nearly two hundred years ago that emotionalism here is king, and can even excuse aberrant behaviour.

A more cheerful example was the solid, well-run Central American airline which was persuaded by its surely youthful PR gang to use the slogan 'Calor, Orgullo y Pasión' – Warmth, Pride and Passion. It was some time before it saw that these might be good stuff in a bridegroom but the last things passengers want in their pilot.

Among the more obtuse of the elite, there is still the legacy of the second and third generation Spanish colonialists who, with none of the courage and hardihood of the first-wave Conquistadores, locked onto the terrain and its peoples and forged the repressive, exploiting mind-set that still remains. The first and absolute priority of the tiny white all-powerful majority in the indigenous countries is to defend their whiteness from the slightest touch of 'native' blood. There is a country club in Guatemala called *Club Mayan Golf*. The only way a true descendant of the Maya, who make up fifty percent of the population, could get in is as a caddy.

Over the years I discovered that the Stalinist communists and the far right elite had one thing in common – they were blinkered. They cannot adapt. The right-wing in the heavily indigenous nations cannot see that the exploited Mayan or Qechua and other majorities will one day take over and if it's not by elections it will be by force without mercy. It is starting now.

I was never to escape the wonder at how the many first class Latins, from field hands to big bankers, who were brave, compassionate, hard-working, and decent, that I came to know, maintained their quality in so stagnant a culture. Mark you, I still live here and don't want to move.

One of them, a fellow passenger, nodded at me. He motioned to the queues at the entrance. "Let me take you through customs and immigration. It can be confusing." Even with his helping hand I got a whiff of Latin officialdom. I hadn't seen anything yet. I was due to pass, seething, through customs and police and army bullying at overland frontiers for the next three decades.

Venezuela was the world's leading oil exporter and leading member of OPEC, the Organization of Petroleum Exporting Countries. It had bauxite, iron ore, coal, and hydroelectric potential. It had social legislation, labour laws, and citizens' rights, already in its statutes, but these were largely ignored. It was a democracy. It had a far-right and a Communist Party both of which had members in Congress. It had just elected the first president in history, Rómulo Betancourt, to last his full term without a coup. And it was a shambles. If you made a step forward with a pay-off you got stopped anyway by a creaking, obdurate bureaucracy that hadn't changed in centuries and still dumped files in the corner for want of shelf space.

What's more, *Shell*, a rich Dutch/British enterprise, was the second oil producer in the country.

Fidel Castro, almost a year as top honcho in Cuba, was sounding his flamboyant revolutionary trumpets loud and clear and the disaffected middle class youth, who have always been the spearhead of revolutions, were getting worked up. For MI6, the brief was not to interfere in local sovereignty and politics, where they stepped carefully, but to scout out what Moscow was up to via Cuba.

Before flying out I had met two old Latin American hands. One said that, having blue eyes, I'd have a high old time there. The other, a better counsellor by far, said, "Don't do anything for us for three months. Get yourself thoroughly settled first under whatever your cover is."

My first case officer had other ideas. He wanted results right away. Still in the hotel at a total loss, and still without the essential government press pass or even a clue how to get it, I ended up buying *El Universal*, a major daily, marking off what looked like likely sources among the stories about politicians, trade union leaders and so on. I knew what the main thrust was but I had no idea whatever about the local scene, who was who, who was old hat, and who to get close to, and what were the issues of the day on a national level.

But there were compensations. My very first contact was low down on the scale. A teachers' union leader had made an inflammatory, far-left revolutionary statement to the press extolling Fidel. He was director of a big state school. I took a taxi. The school building was unpainted cinderblock. To get to his office I had to thread my way through fifty young women doing their PT class on the concrete playground. There was no equipment, no gym clothes. They were lying on towels or sweaters, hands under hips, pedalling their strong, golden legs in the air.

I thought, *Jesus, this isn't going be easy.* I willed my eyes to look to the front but even so, there had never in my life been such a challenging scenario. The girls were in no way put out. Those who looked up at me grinned and I felt heat rush up my face.

A secretary showed me in. I greeted him in academic Cambridge, Tripos 1 Spanish. He accepted me at once, and completely at ease, waved a hand at the playground.

"Not a bit like your schools with gymnasiums and showers, eh?" he said.

A straight newsman would get straight to the point. But from the start I worked out that I would have a set of the expected newsman's questions and put the crucial one in the middle somewhere, unobtrusive. In this case it was something like *'Fidel Castro is going to make a difference, right?'* Off he went into a complete picture of reactions of all sectors to the Cuban revolution. It was thorough but day to day stuff. Anyone, including my case officer, would know it all. But I needed it. That was the sort of probing I'd have done in the three months I didn't get. As it happened, this union man became a valuable link later on.

Work evolved into what I called blanket coverage – everything from government, to army, political parties, industry, trade unions, student factions, the church, the lot. I suggested I would be better employed exclusively chasing Soviet penetration. It was the Cold War after all. No. What I got would add to the pile that would arrive from all sources in HQ. They'd sort it out. They have the whole picture.

I got a scoop, by luck. OPEC had its first meeting in September, 1960 in Baghdad. Security, it was reported, was tight. Conclusions would not be announced for some time. The petroleum companies were biting their nails. I had a drink in a girly bar with a local newsman, a live wire. He was fidgety.

"What's up, amigo?" I said.

He looked round and leaned forward. "I've got the OPEC resolutions."

"Well I'm damned. You going to give them to your paper?"

"Not on your life. My source would cut off my cojones."

"Who knows?"

"Only the guy in the Petroleum Ministry who gave me a copy."

"I'll give you five hundred bolivars for it and send it with an embargo– not to be published until the day before it's announced so you'll be in the clear."

I'd just been to the bank so I slipped him five Bs 100 notes, less than a hundred and twenty dollars.

"Oh boy," he said handing me the rolled-up resolutions from his inside pocket. This stuff was priceless. The case officer for sure took it direct to *Shell*. They would have a clear advantage over their rivals. Unless he gave it to the US giants as well, through CIA friends, that is. But this sort of detail was never passed to me by any of the sixteen case officers I was to work with. MI6 did not play around.

This case officer's tour ended the next year. He had urged me to get a car, a smart little *Thunderbird*, if you please. He must have been thinking benevolently about dashing young agents in a sports car with Miss Universe. He was very smart but unlike his knowing colleague in London, had no conception of how a newspaper stringer lived.

I remembered an in-house doctor who'd vetted me in London. "Don't see many of you Fleet Street chaps in here, you know," he said with a smile that demonstrated he was intrigued to come face to face with one of that dubious breed.

The man who took over damn near drove me into the ground.

First day on the job. Immigration mugshot in Venezuela,
December 1960

*Searching, without machete, for forgotten ladders of
dictator Gomez, at Los Morros, Venezuela, 1964*

Spook at work, Caracas 1966.

Chapter 9

Tanganyika

What didn't drive me into the ground was a little walk around in Tanganyika. I was a subaltern in the Duke of Cornwall's Light Infantry, in Mogadishu, Italian Somaliland, in 1948-49. Off duty, I was training the boxing team for the East Africa Command championships in Nairobi, if we could ever get there, more than eight hundred miles without a yard of asphalt.

There was no gym. We'd form a circle in the sand and number off. Two numbers were called and two men would run into the centre of the ring and batter each other for sixty seconds no matter what their size and weight. If a featherweight failed to attack a heavyweight he'd be sent out of the ring. To start the game, called 'milling' in the army, I went first and one number was called out. He was an old-hand corporal, long-time army welterweight, far stronger than me and 20lbs heavier. I flailed away at him until he put his left glove on the back of my neck and pressed his right into my bent-down face. He stepped back and I pummelled away again but doubt I hit him once.

When the next two were called, I asked him why. He said he could do anything with anyone so open. As I couldn't cover he flipped lefts high on my face too fast for me to block and when I began to duck them came in with his right uppercut that would have mangled me if he hadn't pulled it.

"But go on," he said, "ye'll have a good team."

Another subaltern who had come out from Sandhurst asked to join the ring. He was a freckled redhead, innocent of everything but his family tradition of service, later to get a Military Cross against the Mau Mau. After punching it out with a stalwart Cornishman he joined me and said, astonished, "That man clapped me on the shoulder and said, 'good lad'."

The rains flooded the roads to Nairobi and we missed the jousting. The colonel said the team, for their months of hard training, could go on leave when the road opened. In those days, there was no leave for anyone.

I, with my insignificant, speak-when-spoken-to rank, blurted out, "Can I go with them, sir?"

Utterly confounded, with thirty-three years of silent subalterns behind him, and eyebrows raised to his hairline, he replied, "Well, I suppose so."

There was general disbelief that young Nott was getting away from that sticky hell-hole, but I was already thinking about Kilimanjaro, about two hundred and twenty-five miles further than Nairobi. Knowing nothing whatsoever about the mountain or how to get to it, and with very little money, I persuaded the quartermaster to let me take a few cans of rations which had lost their labels and been set aside. He also lent me a paratrooper smock and a wool cap. I had no sleeping bag.

The road convoy was a string of trucks and buses driven by Italian colonists. Besides the team there were sixty black soldiers, askaris, led by a sergeant from the King's African Rifles, who was due for discharge. I was told I was in charge and to 'get every man to Nairobi'. Camps for the night were normally inside a zariba, a high, thick thorn-bush circle with one entrance, built by travellers against roving Shifta bandits and big animals. A few days out, on high ground before the Juba River the KAR sergeant saluted at first light, smart as hell, and reported three men missing.

"Where'd they go?" I asked, uselessly.

"Over deh. Gone home." He waved his arm over the immense plain below us.

"Did they take their rifles?" *God, let it not be so. We'll be court-martialled.*

"No, sah."

We shared a small, hidden grin of relief. "Let's go then," I said.

That night, after we crossed the Juba, a three-ton truck drew up behind us in the dark.

An immaculate man in top boots and riding breeches dismounted and asked who we were. Then, standing even taller, appeared Col. Richard Meinertzhagen, famous and controversial Great War soldier operating in the Middle East with T.E. Lawrence, OSS man, explorer and scientist. They had travelled through Yemen, Aden, Ethiopia and Somalia. He advised me to go for Mount Kenya, 'much more of a mountain than Kilimanjaro'.

A white-robed servitor in red fez and cummerbund laid a folding table in the road where the colonel and his scientist partner Dr. Phillip Clancey, would eat, 'dine' they would probably call it.

I went back to sit with the drivers who had rigged a sheet on the back of a truck and switched on the headlights of the one behind. We were far better lit than the explorers with their lantern and I ate some bully beef and hardtack biscuits while we cooked for the slow trucks coming up hours later.

The safari truck went ahead next morning. Later, in the last light of day, a driver and the KAR sergeant hushed us with a finger on their lips and slithered off into the bush. We heard shots. They came back with a gerenuk, its long neck trailing. In minutes it was gutted and its heart, liver, and kidneys were crackling and browning in a big iron frying pan on the fire. It was skinned, quartered and roasting on spits ready for the troops in the slow trucks. They could smell it miles away, they said.

Nairobi was a dusty little town. Masai with spears strode the main street, one testicle bulging outside their loincloths. With the boxers settled I got a bus for Arusha and Moshi, take-off point for Kilimanjaro.

At the hotel up in the forest above Moshi the only other guest was an officer's wife and her children. She sewed a button on my shirt. She said encouragingly that she thought I'd get up to the summit and come down with flowers woven round my tepee by the guide as a sign that I'd made it.

The tepee came with the hotel food, and an old time alpenstock. The flowers you had to earn. I told the hotel I didn't need rations, trying to hold down the price, but they left out the blankets too. My guide was Johannes, a thin, serious man in his forties in a long white robe. There were two porters with their rations in wooden boxes on their heads. The trek comprised three huts with less than ten miles between them. You climbed through forest to the first hut, then across open moor to the second hut on the saddle between Kibo and its companion peak Mawenzi, then to the rocks and scree at Kibo Hut, at 15,400ft. We went past the first hut without stopping.

I swatted heavy, grey flies off the porters' bare backs

up to the second hut. Here they dropped their boxes and lay down. Neither Johannes nor I had a watch. I pointed up the track to Kibo Hut, nodding my head. He looked up at the sun and in seconds he had the guides on their feet and away we went. Ignorant of high mountains I knew nothing of acclimatisation or that climbing at that speed was an unfailing invitation to altitude sickness.

At the hut the porters made their rich-smelling supper and I opened the first can I'd brought from Mogadishu. It was peas. I ate half and in the sudden cold of night at 15,400ft, and with no sleeping bag or blankets, got between two stiff mattresses with all my clothes on.

After a few miserable hours Johannes banged on the door. As it turned out it was hours too early but after only a few steps up the scree I was sick as a dog and lost all sense of time. It seemed like 5,000ft of steep rubble where you are as likely to slip back a pace as make one upwards.

I was throwing up all the way to the crater's edge. At one point I was on my knees and even on my back trying to get up a little of the scree on my elbows. The whole of Africa could hear my retching and groaning. I had glimpses of Johannes standing over me, black against the stars, waving his alpenstock upwards and shouting 'keep going', or something like it, in Swahili.

On the crater rim, still night and around zero, we hunched down between two rocks and I got the fags out. We sat there for a long time smoking. There was no wind or we would have frozen. With first light we touched each other's shoulder in relief and went on the rest of the way to the summit, which was then called Kaiser Wilhelmspitze. We got there as dawn broke having taken about twenty-one hours to complete a trek normally of four or five days. Across the crater the ice towers of the glacier, much bigger than it is now, glittered. All Africa was below us. A sea of cloud, thousands of feet down, gold and oyster shell in the sun, spread to the horizon, Mount Meru towering above it. There was an iron chest with a big, ancient ledger for climbers to sign their names. I added my name but with a splitting head and still nauseous, I failed to note any of the names and dates. We turned back and raced down the best scree run I know of and one that put me in good fettle. We stopped at the hut. The porters were already packed up. I opened another tin and it was a sort of pudding which I ate cold. We reached the second hut and passed it with Johannes looking at me quizzically and then approvingly.

At the first hut I found a well-equipped mountaineer, and a tall youth enjoying a savoury porter-cooked stew. The climber was 'Baron' Kramm, ex-special forces and now Resident Magistrate in Nairobi. He said he doubted the tall youth would make it and asked if I would go up again with him if he paid the food and porters. I ran down the seven-odd miles to the hotel, taking off my tepee and its garland of flowers before going in.

And there she was, my glowing matriarch.

"You're back already?" she said with what looked like disappointment. Then she reached for the tepee and saw the flowers. She said, "Well done. How did you do that? It must be a record time." I told her I would be going up again the next day. She looked at me with a range of feelings crossing her face.

Again with Johannes, I caught up with the baron at the second hut. The youth was going down. Next day we went on easily to Kibo Hut, ate and slept until about midnight. I made it up easily this time and at the crater looked down for Kramm. He was so far down it took me time to realize he was retreating. I went on to the summit, and then ran down to the hut. Kramm said he needed more acclimatization and why don't we have a look at Mawenzi. This is a climber's peak, seven miles east. He had a rope but I had army boots with steel plate heel and toe and hobnails in the sole.

Made for falling off rock climbs. We tried several routes up volcanic gullies and finally made it to a ridge that would bring us closer to the final climb to the summit. Johannes, whom we'd left at the hut, made a sudden, biblical appearance further up the ridge in his white shroud, waving his alpenstock in disapproval. It was getting late anyway so we turned back down a lumpy scree of volcanic rocks designed for twisting ankles.

My time was up. We parted on the saddle, Kramm to

go back to Kibo, me to the first hut. Next day I got down to Moshi and found there was no bus. A conversation in the bar and I landed with a District Commissioner who had spent two months of his leave putting trout into the streams on Kilimanjaro and was driving up to Nairobi on his way to a final month fishing in Norway.

Heading north across the game reserve we were the only vehicle, the only humans, and saw every animal it had. By chance an ostrich was in the middle of the dirt road and, confused, chose to run in front of the truck in the same direction.

We watched in astonishment as he sprinted faster and faster a foot ahead of the radiator, shedding feathers, and howled when we found that the speedometer wasn't working to clock his speed. We stopped at a big game hunters' lodge. After a few drinks a white hunter said with quite awful drama that he lived some way up the hill behind the lodge and that he never knew, at night, if he'd get there alive. What would get him, he said, was not a lion or a leopard, but a water buffalo, the most dangerous of all animals.

In Nairobi the convoy was assembled and we were off. There were three trucks, one for the boxers, two with unspecified cargo. Two days out a big black driver produced a very old, tiny, venerable Indian in turban and robes from a cargo truck.

"This is my father," he said, earnestly.

The old man, humbly but with dignity, held out a chipped wash basin and an enamel mug as an offering. I could see on his face his injured pride and the urgency of his appeal. I was twenty and out of my depth. The battalion transport officer, a forceful captain, who had the habit, after ten gins, of having me read to him from the *Ingoldsby Legends* by lantern in his tent while the legs of his canvas chair sank deeper into the sand, would have booted the old man out, roaring with rage, and put the driver on a charge. I hesitated while they both waited, not speaking.

"I can't take your gift because I haven't seen you," I said.

He mumbled something. The driver, beaming, lifted him into the truck and looked back at me. "He tells you, go with God," he said. I never saw the old boy leave the convoy.

We were several miles out of Mogadishu when that same captain, alerted by our dust trail, drove out to meet us. Looking over the backboard of a cargo truck he saw a black woman and child, with coloured dress and turban, maybe Kikuyu or Wacamba. I hadn't seen them. He roared. He said he would dump them there in the bush. I said that as he surely had to get back to the lines I would undertake to drop them at the first shanties on the outskirts without a soul seeing us. I pleaded. I calmed him. He got into his truck and wagged a finger at me.

"If you're caught they'll throw the book at you, both

brigade and battalion standing orders. Now, understand I know nothing about it. You are on your own."

I was to hear that again. Twelve years later.

On Kilimanjaro, 1949

Chapter 10

Parachute

I got out of the doorway of the small, high-wing monoplane and stood one foot on top of the other on the small landing wheel, both hands on the strut under the wing. We were at a thousand two hundred feet over a disused Venezuelan airstrip. The pilot signalled and I pushed off backwards. I counted to four.

The parachute didn't open.

I thought about it for two seconds more and in the dumbest move of my life, counted to four again.

The parachute didn't open.

The 'chute had come out of the pack and streamed upwards without opening. It's called a Roman candle and is fatal unless you have an emergency 'chute. I'd been too strung out about the jump that I didn't take in the pilot's fingers counting to four in front of my face, wordless above the engine noise, and snatching across his chest as if pulling the D-ring opener of the emergency 'chute. I'd never worn one and this was all the training I got. I didn't open it. Didn't even think about it.

But I had a queer flashing thought about the parachute packer, the wild boy of the group who wore a yellow overall so they called him 'cambur'- banana, reportedly smuggling guns from Cuba to the still small guerrilla groups. He'd been impossible to corner for weeks and that's why I was here on this escapade with a bad chute twelve hundred feet up.

I looked down and all was still. I felt I was floating. Suddenly the ground started to rush up at about 120mph…

Special Forces had said nothing about this. I had trained with the 21st SAS at RAF Abingdon in 1953. There were no emergency 'chutes strapped to your chest then, just the one on your back. More recent paratroopers go suddenly quiet when reminded about those primitive days. You can see them picturing it.

When we got to the RAF base there was low cloud and unbelievably a man dropped out of it and then another more or less horizontal as if sleeping, or dead. Then their parachutes opened one after another. They were jumping from a balloon at about six hundred feet. They were in a fool's heaven, we soon learned. They couldn't see the ground before jumping.

As the days went on we debated what was most frightening. Many opted for The Fan.

Thirty feet up in a hangar was a catwalk with a gap in the railing. Here was a circular fan and a miserable ribbon of thin tape. You clipped it loosely round your waist and the instructor, down below, instead of shouting "Go" to galvanize you into action, said calmly, "Go when you're ready. Don't take all day." And you went, straight down to the concrete floor. The resistance of the fan to the air was fiendishly calculated to slow you just before you hit.

But the balloon was the Big Fright. They were old barrage balloons from the war with a cage hanging from them, with a roof and three walls of green canvas from waist level up and a metal strip on the edge of the floor at the exit. The trainees stood around the walls until called over to the door.

The instructor would say, "Starboard exit, red on, stand in the door. Right hand on the wall of the exit, left hand gripping your trousers in front to stop your arms flailing about in the slipstream when you jump from a plane." He would pull you around to get you right and then, "Look down. Put the toe of your boot over the edge. Look down and check it."

You couldn't look down at your foot without looking down the whole six hundred feet to the ground with tiny dots for men and miniature trucks. So you are in a wide-open door, sixty floors up with nothing to hold onto. Silence without the hullabaloo and noise of an aircraft jump. I watched the man before me sagging, his legs buckling with fright, the instructor peering at his face ready to drag him back and fail him. Then a fierce shout, "Green on. GO." He went. I followed, shaking too.

Later we went through this with either a big bag of gear and ammo, with a slot into which your leg fitted and strapped in, or the alternative, a Bren machine gun. I got the Bren gun. I'm a bit of a shorty and the muzzle was almost in my armpit. When you get close to the ground you pull a pin and the bag or gun falls below you to the end of its rope so you don't hit the ground with it still tied on. In jumps as low as six hundred feet there's hardly time to look at the scenery. One thinks of skydivers in blue Lycra and goggles, with their hands free, spread-eagled and smiling. I was called to the door and moved there, pace, thump, pace, thump like Long John Silver. I could feel the gun was a bit loose. I put my left foot on the strip, and looked down unhappily. The 'GO' sounded and I swung my right leg forward and out. The butt plate of the Bren hit the metal strip and I cartwheeled out, arms waving. I was till turning when the chute opened. I let the gun go and landed with a bang, tried to do the paratrooper roll, failed and bonked my helmet on the hard ground. I turned face down to haul on the rigging to spill the air out of the 'chute. I looked up to see the chief instructor in RAF blue examining me.

"You get your rigging twisted maybe when you tumble around in the slipstream on an aircraft jump," he said.

I stood up in silence. "But *you* got five twists in a *balloon* jump," he said, turning away.

Sure to God, he'll fail me, I thought. But there was the ghost of a grin on his leathery mug.

None of this had readied me for falling at round 120mph into rocks and trees and dry hard ground. At the very last moment I flipped over to see what was going on above me and the 'chute opened with a crack, the harness bit into my groin and I landed with legs open like a frog.

By the time the instructor and the jeep got to me I saw my left leg was bent at a revolting angle. Miraculously, without pain, I seized my foot and my lower leg and pushed the fracture ends together in a grip that I never relaxed until they'd got me in the jeep, transferred me to the small plane, flown me to Caracas, and got me into a car and to the clinic. During the flight I found I could move the two pieces of my leg slightly but visibly, bending it. I waited until the instructor, an old friend, next to the pilot, looked back at me. I showed him this obscene trick, grinning. He paled and turned away and, not for the first time, mouthed, "Bloody British." What he meant was, "Bloody lucky British."

A few days later in my bed, the cast on my leg bloody because they'd split the Achilles tendon to screw in a couple of pins, and in a foul mood, I had a visitor. Sat gingerly on the end of my bed, crestfallen, was Cambur.

Nott tangled in a tree after descent by rope from helicopter seen above. Special Forces seeking how to drop men in jungle are welcome to try this.

Chapter 11

Santo Domingo

"If the secret police get you and start pulling your fingernails out, don't look for us for help. We'll disown you. You are on your own."

It was my tall, heavy, pinstriped, and affable, second case officer talking. I'd told him how a hard-eyed colonel whom I was trying to get close to had a 9mm Browning on his glass-topped desk and had twirled it with his finger so that it was pointing at me. I thought it was just a bit of in-house macho talk that might amuse him. But he was serious and leaned forward in his chair wagging a finger at me for emphasis.

My first thought was, *What's this 'us'? What was I? A mere auxiliary and expendable at that?* I thought I was now one of these urbane chaps who have 'luncheon' at White's. A member of an ancient and revered service. I'd seen somewhere that our cousins, the CIA, called their locally recruited sources, 'little farts'. You know, natives. But I was an English native. I decided, wrongly as I see it now, that it was not the sort of question one asked. Neither would it be appreciated if I said, 'now you tell me'. Next I felt a perverse pride that I was in such a hard-assed outfit and went back to my *Glenfiddich*, nodding to him to say I knew it all along, of course.

This was high season in the Cold War. Slogans in the western world included 'Better Red Than Dead' i.e. better succumb to an aggressive Soviet Union and fall under the communist yoke than be evaporated or burnt or mutilated or given cancer in a nuclear war. This was the defeatists' line. The rest, the majority, went about their business with the constant question of whether they should have children, or struggle for success, or look to the future in any way. Soviet Premier Nikita Khrushchev after all, in October 1960, took off his shoe, banged it on the podium at the United Nations and told the West, "We will bury you."

An agent's function as I saw it, was, apart from other calls, to lift stones and find communists, particularly in my case, Cubans or their allies, funded and trained by Moscow and infiltrated into the left-wing of whatever country I was in. This meant penetrating that left-wing. The further the agent penetrated the more excuse the gendarmes would have for giving him the treatment if they caught him. I mean, they had a job to do, also.

This Gestapo operated in all the countries I covered apart from the Caribbean islands, and was known by various acronyms, DISIP, DIGEPOL, DIT, DINE and so on.

This situation became clearer as the 60's developed. At the same time there was another lesson: don't underestimate a contact, cultivate him and await the chain effect. Cambur. He admitted there was no arms supply to Stalingrad in the Central University, which clicked with my own onsite prowling later on. It made a 'negative report' which were never believed if they concerned a bee in the bonnet of some higher up, especially with the cousins.

"We think you ought to go and take another look," was the dread response which involved retracing a prickly trail all over again. But he came up with an introduction to a Communist Party member, very smart, with access to the top leaders Eduardo Machado, Jesús Faría, Pompeyo Marquez and Teodoro Petkoff, but who kept out of the limelight, a serious part of his usefulness. He was also a serious whiskey drinker and from the start, we got along.

The Party launched guerrilla tactics in the early 60's at a time when the population wasn't ready for it and as a consequence was outlawed, three of its top leaders captured and locked up in San Carlos barracks' prison. My friend went underground. We met when we could, with great caution. In a smallish one-room pub one night we sat at the bar watching behind us in the mirror as we talked. The door banged open and a patrol of the National Guard, armed to the teeth, filed in and stood along the wall opposite us.

Before they had started anything, my lad, pale and flustered, pulled out an identity card, held it up and said too loudly, "I've got a card. Here it is. Here's my card."

"Get your bloody arm down and shut up," I hissed.

It was enough. He recovered in a flash and we both turned round to watch, our faces reflecting what any honest citizen would: surprise, alarm, curiosity. A hard-faced lieutenant with the patrol, Gestapo, walked round peering at the customers, one by one. He got to us and gave us the same stare. I nodded slightly and smiled slightly, approvingly even; after all, he was there to protect us from the Red Army. He kept his faintly sneering, menacing face on. That was the sign that he was a tough hombre. He waved the soldiers out and left.

We breathed out, both of us in a tizzy. I asked my friend to show me his identity card. It was for somebody else.

"Who?" I said.

"He's missing."

He returned my helping hand with a request. I was to meet a third party in an open air café and help him. He was from the Dominican Republic and wanted me to put a 'heavy box' in the boot of my car and take him to deliver it. Keen to get in among these fellows I said, yes.

At night he guided me through a maze of Caracas

streets. He made a few double-backs and circles, which gave the game away. He was putting me off the scent. Eventually he said to back into a vehicle entrance to a big building. It was a police station. He went into a side door, came out and beckoned me into an unlit corner. We hoisted a heavy wooden box about three or four feet long, about a foot and a half square, and put it into the back of my car. He was sizzling with triumph. He just couldn't contain it. He lifted the lid and said, "Look."

They were submachine guns neatly packed in thick grease.

This didn't fit at all with a police station so I patted him on the shoulder in congratulation and said, "Are we leaving now?"

He guided me on an even more intricate route until he stopped me in a street of small houses and no lights. We lifted the box onto the pavement. He took my arm, thanked me, handed me a name and telephone number on a scrap of paper, and asked me to drive off.

He had done his job well. I had no idea where I was.

Next day I telephoned the number. It was a quietly-spoken doctor of about fifty. He was in exile from the Dominican Republic where he was in danger from the army goons for his affiliation with Juan Bosch, the reformist leader elected president of that country in February 1963 and thrown out after only seven months in office by the right-wing army backed by the landowners, business and the church. He had won the presidency in the first free elections there in history. His platform was to right the wrongs enforced by the thug dictator Leonidas Trujillo who had held the country down for thirty-one years until his assassination in 1961. The doctor gave me a masterly run-down on the situation and said, "By the way, did you know Bosch's son is in Caracas?" He gave me a telephone number.

This fifth link in the chain was a high-spirited young man. Just how high I was to discover the night he came to my flat for a whiskey session with friends.

An old flame from my London days who was visiting a huge hacienda in Colombia had flown in in time for the party. She was surrounded by males. It was time for a stunt. The wide picture windows in my flat rolled back into the wall. There was a metal railing but no terrace. You stood in the living room and looked straight down ten floors. In between flats the walls were cinder-block lattices so air and light got into the kitchens.

I'd noted before that you could get onto the lattice by a wide step from the railing. I shouted, "Watch this now," or some such rubbish, made the dicey swing across to the lattice and climbed down the ten floors. I ran to the swimming pool, dived in, picked a blossom off a shrub, put it in my teeth, ran back and swarmed up the lattice to the howls and shouts of the gang. I swung over the railing, knelt on one knee before Josephine and said, "For you, angel."

She surveyed my dripping self and turned away. "Oh, grow up," she said.

Young Bosch, however, was enthusiastic. At first light, with most of the party gone, he urged me to do it again with him. So we did. What's more, we didn't stop at the flat on the way up but continued two floors further up, pulled over a nasty ledge sticking out two feet, got onto the roof and found the door to the fire staircase. He was ecstatic. He'd never done anything like that in his life, he said. More power to him. Before he left he gave me the telephone number of his house in Puerto Rico.

"You never know," he said.

In 1965 there was an uprising against the gang who had ousted Juan Bosch. Arms were handed out in the city centre. The pro-Bosch Constitutionalists held their positions against the army. But there was confusion. The leader of the rising was a Colonel Francisco Caamaño, a career officer but a reformist later to be executed by the army.

Nobody knew who, or what groups, were getting into the fight in order to gain political leverage. Given the Cold War context Washington and its allies had to assume the communists were mixed up in it. Given that context they could not afford to take the risk of 'another Cuba'. The marines landed joined by the 82nd Airborne. The rebels were cut off in their portion of the city.

I booked the Dominican airline flight for the next

morning. There was a crowd at the airline's counter and a lot of shoving and shouting. I got through and was told the plane had already gone. First time I'd known a flight to leave *early*.

"But I have a reservation and a ticket," I said.

"So has everyone," the man said. "When the plane filled up, it left. Flights are now suspended."

Back in Caracas the doctor advised I should fly to Puerto Rico and go to the Dominican consul's office. There was a crowd there too. I got no welcome from the functionary I saw. I couldn't work out if he was a junta man or a Bosch supporter. The distinction was crucial. He said unkindly that they'd send my passport details to Santo Domingo and I must wait for permission. If I got it. I had the excruciating vision of telling my case officer that I failed to get in. But I had an ace in hand, the doctor's card with young Bosch's number. I called, and he welcomed me to his house where I met his famous father. The cogs were set to running and the next day I had my visa. What's more, I also got the telephone number for an extreme left group who had popped out of clandestinity when the goons withdrew after failing to take the rebel positions.

What I didn't have was accreditation to a newspaper. This was getting to be a problem. Wangling my way in repeatedly was no longer a thing to grin about but a nerve wringer. I got to the only hotel, which was used by the Americans to evacuate nationals and others who wanted out. It also housed the foreign newspapermen. I found the press office to get a press card. The man opened a big ledger where I saw, across the desk and upside down, the list of newsmen who had signed in. He asked what paper I was with. If I claimed a newspaper and there was already a reporter from it there, or was coming, I'd be hounded not only by the authorities but by the newsmen. Looking covertly down the list I saw that the *Daily Telegraph* was missing.

"*Daily Telegraph,*" I said. This is a Fleet Street heavy of great prestige. My original accreditation note, typed on a half letter-sized page, was five years old, and worn out.

At any moment the real man could turn up.

That night I went to the 82nd Airborne's sand-bagged machine gun nest which marked the gap in the line you could go through at your own risk. Beyond was a stretch of open ground. I showed my press pass and the soldiers avowed they favoured the rebels over the junta as they waved me through. Once across the waste lot I asked passers-by for the address I was going to. It was close. I could walk there. I knocked on the door of a small house. A girl answered the door and said to wait. It was a good ten minutes.

She took me down the street to a big cinder-block building; a school or a community hall. She showed me the door and left me. She was off-handed about the occasion. She said, "He'll see you now," with no enthusiasm. She was no fired-up revolutionary groupie, I noted. I went in. There a large hall, a stage with a revolutionary banner and not a soul in sight.

A young fellow appeared on stage, thin, heavily bespectacled, in old army drabs, a file of papers in hand. He marched to the table centre-stage without looking my way and sat rigidly looking straight to his front. I got his number right away. This was the zealot revolutionary, intense, sure of his new faith, unassailable in his importance as one of its priests. He looked like a stiff North Korean party commissar. I got onto the stage, stood in front of him and said, "Press." He waved to a chair. I knew how it would go.

I'd ask him a harmless question that gave him an opening to spout. He would go on about the workers, social justice, and death to the oppressors. So it went. He banged the desk. He stood up to attention at the word, 'La Revolución'. He sat breathing deeply and I thanked him, nodding in approval. In the next hour of leading him on I was sure that it was a small group, not united with others in a front. There was no front; the Marxist groups did not form an armed unit in the struggle. A few individuals had got weapons when the Constitutionalist rebels had seized a sector of the town and handed them out.

He himself had none. When I asked for contact with his fellow revolutionary groups he wouldn't, or couldn't, come across. I should go to Caamaño's headquarters.

"They'll be there," he said.

Next day at the headquarters Caamaño was away but there were plenty of unidentifiable types moving around, inside and in the street. I spent the morning weaving around, doing my earnest reporter bit. I found nothing to shake my impression. I came back the next day. I had to have some more sources for my report.

What I got was more of the same.

Back in the hotel I had to face up to the cover problem. At the press office I asked, gossipy, if there was anyone new I might know. There wasn't, yet. I had to weigh the possibility of getting blown against my confidence that I had enough for a report. Stay and get more stuff or get out while the going was good?

That night, a television news team manager, or someone like it, invited me to his room for a drink. He was grey-haired and no fool. He said he was always alert for interlopers in the Press crowd. Like CIA men, or whatever. The Press owed it to themselves to weed them out. They could damage the whole media.

"How come we don't see you in the bar? We're all there at night," he said, with a sort of phoney concern.

It was time for a show. I told him I couldn't agree more. They are a menace to the media. If it gets out, no one will believe newsmen. We'll look like fools, too, investigative reporters who can't smell a rat. I went on for some time and then launched into small talk, like, I don't know how I'm to get out of here. The airline is screwed up. I'm done here and want to get back to London. He pondered this for a moment. I don't know if he was thinking, 'let's help this guy or let's get rid of him'.

"We have a Cessna going to Puerto Rico every day with our stuff. You could go on that tomorrow."

In London I got a hotel, asked room service for a whiskey and a ham sandwich every hour and got down to writing it all out. Get to the point, short sentences, no fancy words, Anglo-Saxon, not Latinised.

The next day I had a Cuban safe house to look into.

It's only orange juice, Minister. It will help you remember. Caracas 1965.

Chapter 12

Salvador 216

"Get out now! Run for it! Your contact was shot in the street," he was shouting down the phone and then hung up.

But when was he shot? Today? Yesterday? Did he have my name on him? My room number? Was he shot dead or did the goons beat it out of him before he died? This was El Salvador at the peak of the dirty war against the guerrillas.

Five days before, a four-man Dutch news television crew were seized by the army and shot. They'd probably criticized the death squads or called the guerrillas 'freedom fighters'. The military knew their own record was atrocious and well broadcast internationally. Most of them didn't give a damn. I had a vision of telling a seething colonel interrogating me about my link to the guerrillas. 'Well, I have to get both sides of the story, you see. It's just my job...'

I had located the Mexico City HQ of one of the Salvadorean guerrilla groups in an office on La Reforma. High priced real estate. A disgruntled Salvadorean right-winger, a backer of death squads, and with one of his own on his estate, had told me with contempt that the Mexicans had a bargain with Castro to allow Central American guerrilla groups to run offices there unhampered. In return, Castro would not back a guerrilla movement in Mexico. That made sense, a hardnosed Castro manoeuvre.

I'd finally persuaded the Salvadoreans I was sympathetic to their fight and to get me up to one of their guerrilla camps in the mountains. This was a prime target – scouting for Soviet-type weapons, Cuban advisers, Nicaraguan supply lines and so on.

I was to go to San Salvador, the capital, put up at the *Hotel Camino Real,* call the Mexico office from the public exchange and give the number of my room. No name, place, time. Then I would stay in my room until the contact came. I had driven the twelve hundred miles from Mexico City at top speed, average 75mph, thinking I'd got it made... and now this.

I stood in the door of the telephone office for a while thinking it out, looking up and down the street. But only for a moment. I crossed over to the hotel. "Don't run,

Nott," I said. I went up to my room, and threw everything in my bag. Then I went down the fire stairs to the lobby. I handed in the key to my room, number 216.The desk clerk reached under the counter. I watched him closely but he didn't lift the telephone, or make any signal that I could see. If the army had figured that 216 was a hotel room number, they'd have checked the three big hotels, and waited for me here in the lobby. They would then hustle me out as they did the Dutch newsmen. The clerk would have been terrorized to signal when he identified me. He returned to where I was. He smiled. "Enjoyed your stay, señor?"

I nodded to him, signed the bill and left, walking to the street door, longing to run, and got in my car. I drove slowly across the car park, not knowing where to go. Airport no, that was a trap. The frontier wouldn't do either. By the time I got there they'd have my name and passport number from the hotel register and I'd be stopped.

Then I remembered where the Dutch crew had stayed and the straw I grasped at was the one about lightning not striking in the same place twice. What's more, it was a small hotel, no room 216 there. Pathetic, but it was all I could think of. "*Hotel Alameda,*" I told myself, turning right on the street.

It was downmarket from the *Camino Real*. The lobby was small and there was no one about. I went to reception and asked for a room. The clerk considered the keys on a board behind him.

"We're almost full," he said.

"Terrible thing about those television men," I said, feeling my way.

Discreetly, glancing around, he muttered that they'd been a nice bunch.

"Is their stuff still here?"

"No. Their embassy took it away this morning."

"And their rooms?"

"They're ready again." He shrugged, a personal apology for such commercialism. I saw now where he was at.

"I'll take one of them if you're full," I said. "It's okay by me."

He looked at me for a moment with no expression, asked to see my passport, entered the number in the register and gave me a key. I took my bag to the room and feeling trapped, came down to the bar across from reception. I was still pondering what to do when, with no ceremony, an army patrol barged in and asked the receptionist for the visitors' register. I froze. By the time I had unfrozen and walked unobtrusively out of reception and down the steps to the street, the patrol was following me. I came to a halt waiting for a shout and a gun muzzle in the back. But they veered off to their jeep without even looking my way.

I went back to reception. The man who had signed me in and seen the whole performance, said, deadpan, "Sí, señor, en qué puedo servirle?" *What can I do for you?*

"They were looking for someone?"

"I don't know. They come every night to check the register." *Every night.*

"Thanks."

Back in the bar I thought it over. They'd had up to two nights. Just now they had my name and passport number right in front of them. They could have got them from the *Camino Real* after I had left. They couldn't have been looking for them. Maybe they were looking for someone else and missed me. They couldn't be that dumb. Maybe they still hadn't worked out what the number was. My answer was a small hotel. For the moment.

More holes in it than a sieve but it was all I had. Except for luck.

Chapter 13

Freight Train

The huge locomotive thundered round the bend on a high embankment, in a cloud of steam. The garish light from its open firebox flickered red on the black smoke billowing above it. Aged fifteen, a schoolboy, I crouched in the frosted grass, and watched it roar past. Then I ran up the slope. I had to get there and onto the train before the guard's van came up and I was spotted. Near Wavertree Station, Liverpool, I had climbed the palisade of old railway sleepers, careful with the spikes on top, and dropped down the other side. There was a ruined shed smelling of tar. I'd got inside out of the wind and filled my pipe with soggy tobacco from cigarette butts I'd picked up in the street. This was my Everest Pipe, part of the dream of being with those climbers puffing away at dusk outside their bivouac.

Truth is I was nervous as always waiting for the first

freight train to come round that bend high on my right. From experience I knew the sounds, the freewheeling clank of the lone bull engine without wagons, the smooth speed of the passenger train and, what I was waiting for this time, the grinding, heavy pull of a long, loaded freight.

Here it was, and now as I faced it came the fearful excitement. There was a two-foot bed of stones, then the sleepers, then the rails, the wheels and then the high wooden sides of the wagons, their lowest point level with my chest. They roared past each hitting me with a whoosh of air. Then I saw a low flat-bed rushing up, the only chance to get on a train moving so fast.

I stepped in close, flung my left arm blindly over the steel edge, grabbed a cable tie-down as it slammed into my hand and was jerked belly-up off the ground. I jack-knifed and twisted over the edge to land with a bang face down on the steel plate floor. Still tightly holding the cable which for once was not frayed and spiky, I got to my knees and whooped with triumph. I'd jumped the fastest freight yet. I was a hard man hobo, battered but on my way.

I was soon leaving Liverpool and into a garish industrial hell of huge sheds below the embankment, shrieking jets of steam, poison green and silver pools of effluent, stink of chemicals, and the roaring pullulating of a pounding night shift. I yelled in exhilaration as the train thundered through and out into the fields.

Shivering in my soaked clothes I had to get out of the flat-bed or freeze. In front was a high box car. I could jump the gap to the ladder rungs. Or feel my way across from one buffer to the next, a dangerous manoeuvre because they could smash together at any moment if the engine slowed suddenly, and jerk apart again with appalling violence. I'd not been caught yet because I had early learned to listen for the clanging echoing down the line of trucks. In any case, I didn't like the idea of skittering across the ice on the roof of a high box car with nothing to hold on to.

To the rear was a wagon with a tarpaulin. I stood on the buffer and leaned across to grasp it, frozen and hard. I stepped over and burrowed under it out of the knifing wind. It was full of heavy wooden crates and the respite ended there and then as I felt them grind and shift. Get your foot between two of them and you'd lose it.

I crawled over them, keeping my fingers out of the gaps, and peered out. In the starlight I could see another open truck with no tarpaulin. I crossed over quickly and ducked into a corner, curling up. It would have to do. It's empty and that's bad news. When it shunts you're thrown from front to back and to front again, scraping along the splintery floor.

But we're out in the country now and making good steady speed. I tried to doze. Too cold by far. No gloves, no scarf, and no anorak just a jersey and jacket. I'd only one shilling and sixpence to get back to Liverpool from wherever the hell this thing was going. I wouldn't get far on that.

Where was it going, then? Goods wagons, I'd discovered, had a steel spring, like a rat trap, on the beam under the walls, over the wheels. It held in place a docket showing the destination for the wagon and cargo. I hitched myself over the edge, one hand and one foot hooked on top. One leg dangling, one arm reaching down to fumble with the clip, not a thing you normally open with one hand. Two fingers on the spring, thumb against the beam and two fingers to grab the docket.

I recalled yelping as a train thundered into a tunnel while I was doing this. I tried to flatten myself against the wagon-side coughing in the smoke, head ringing from the roaring noise bouncing back off the walls. But now I had the docket and swung back up into the wagon. In the corner I huddled over it and struck a match. Manchester, it said. Good God, a city. Once I got into it I'd have a hard time getting out. Maybe I should drop off if the train slowed. In any case, I went back over the side to replace the docket. I couldn't get some poor bloody railwayman into trouble.

I raised my head. By God, it was slowing. Worse, it stopped. I looked over the side. Black night, stars, dark fields. I could get off and trudge over them to a road. But which way would I go? And there's hours to daylight.

Suppose a police car went by as I trudged along in the dead of night? What to say to them?

It was then I heard the first footstep. Someone was crunching along the gravel at the side of the track. Someone with a lantern. The guard, for God's sake.

I ducked and waited. Could he have seen the flare of my match?

Could he have marked the wagon and was coming for me? The heavy steps crunched nearer until they were alongside. I stopped breathing. Then the loudest, most majestic fart in all England that night was let go by the guard who thought he was far from all men. He grunted a contented 'ah' and without a pause walked on, going to see the engine crew.

I then had a dose of what I called 'the siding syndrome'. When a train stops in the middle of nowhere, in silence, you have to keep quiet and not move. You have no idea how long it will be there. You are anxious to get wherever it is going before daybreak so you can escape from the stockyards in the dark. But if you get off and walk until you find a road and then a fork, which one to choose?

I wanted to get back somewhere close and maybe use my pennies for a bus part of the way back to Liverpool. I didn't want to go all the way to Manchester. Walking out of a city is difficult and once out there would be forty more miles to go.

I had to get off before too long or dawn would come and I'd get trapped in a stockyard in daylight. I had no watch. But I never thought of possessions out of my reach. Make do with what you've got. Play the life game with the cards you were dealt and don't complain. Inner resource. I didn't think about all that stuff either. Hadn't heard any of it yet. Listen. It's the footsteps again. The guard was going back to his van. We'd be moving shortly. The train jerked forward, the wagons clanging, and picked up speed. It kept it up for what seemed like hours and I was stuck aboard. There was no jumping off at this speed.

In the grey, predawn gloom I saw I was in a town, roofs black against the sky. Manchester and a huge stockyard. On the left was a high, black-tarred brick wall. On the right seventy yards of crisscrossing rails then a high embankment topped with a rail-sleeper fence with a row of terrace houses behind it. The train slowed momentarily and this time I did not hesitate. Over the side I hung from my left hand and put the other in front of my chest against the wood ready to push off and drop. I peered down urgently to see what was below. Often there were old rails, or cables in metal grooves, switching gear, fearful things to drop onto, which could trap your feet, break your ankles, or bring you down on your face with a bang. I landed hard, tumbling forward onto my knees.

But I'd been seen. Railwaymen, with shunting poles, long heavy things with a hook on the end, were running towards me shouting. I sprang up and raced across the rails, up the bank and was over the six-foot spiked fence before they could get near me. I dropped on the other side into the back yard of one of a row of houses. Trapped. The men were puffing up the slope, yelling, "Stop him!"

I tried the back door of the house whose yard I'd dropped into. It opened and I was in the kitchen. I went through another door into a bare room with a sack of potatoes against the wall. I stepped through the next door and faced a family having their Sunday breakfast. Everyone froze. Nobody spoke. I raced to the door to the street clawing at the bolts, turned the knob and it opened. I leaped into the street, turned left and ran like the wind. Nothing like fright to get you moving. I was going so fast I had to curve out into the crossroad at the end in order to turn left again. In a few blocks I stopped and leaned against a wall retching, my breath ragged. I would not get far running in a city street. Purse snatcher.

I made myself walk and followed the road which got busier as I went. I saw a bridge ahead and the river and a figure at a bus stop looking at me curiously. He was a fine, strapping buck in his big camel-hair overcoat wide open to show his dandy suit and long white scarf, his trilby on the back of his head. A pretty girl was leaning her head against his arm.

"Is there a bus to Liverpool?" I asked him, smiling a bit light-headedly wanting somehow not an answer but to get close to health and cleanliness and good cheer.

"No, but there's a train," the man said.

"What's the fare?" I asked.

"It's a few bob I'd reckon."

I laughed, shrugged and turned away.

"What's up?" the man said. "No money? Take this. The station's up there. You better run."

I took the two half crowns and sprinted off turning to wave and say thanks, thank you, thank you again. At the station I thought, *It's early morning, you're going to ride all the way back like a sissy? Starving?* I bought a small chocolate bar and a quarter pint of milk cold in its glass bottle and with an inch of cream on top. In the street I thought twice about asking which way is Liverpool. I looked at the shadows and saw the sun was behind me so I was facing west and all I had to do was walk that way. "Follow the bus route," I said. It took me three hours to the first fields although it felt like six.

I trudged on, soon getting into the rhythm of my Foreign Legion forced march, a longer stride than you could normally keep up unless you're trained. Head down, feet just brushing the ground as you swung forward, close your mind to tiredness, empty stomach, thirst, cold, the dirt, scratches and bruises of the night and say march, march, march like a quiet drumbeat in your head. Miles up the road there were houses and a pub in its gardens. There was a heavy truck parked with a high load covered by tarpaulin.

The driver's cab was empty. I lay in the grass and waited. But I slept, briefly, and woke to the revving of the motor. I watched it back out onto the road and heard it change gear. I sprinted up behind it as it accelerated and leaped to grab the tailboard, swarm up the tarp and hide in a fold on top. Behind me the driver of a following car shook his fist at me.

About an hour later the truck turned right and I lifted my head. *Jesus, where's it going?* I thought of banging on the cab roof so the driver would stop but feared he'd give me a crack on the ear.

Just then the truck slowed to pick up a soldier with a girl. I heard a cheery shout, "Where you going, mate?" and the dismaying reply, "Preston."

I slithered off the back and stepped onto the pavement. The driver saw me and jumped out. "Where the 'ell did you come from, you little bugger?" he shouted.

I backed away, hands in front. "Can you just tell me the way to Liverpool?" I said. The driver waved his arm. "Get the 'ell away from this truck, d'ye hear?"

I turned back along the road. It was the same as always. Drivers or passers-by who would give a lift or a direction to a soldier, very rarely helped a boy, dirty and with torn clothes. Escaped from borstal, they'd be thinking. Juvenile delinquent. That's what you get for being a little shorty looking like you were twelve.

"You're on your own," I told myself. "You'll get no

help from anyone." I got into my pace, footsore, march, march, march. Some miles further, going up a hill, a milk tanker passed me slowly. In a trice I was after it, jumping onto the big brass tap on the back which had a step under it as a foothold. I twisted sideways, got a leg over the tap and held on to the round handle not quite sure that I could stay in place and wondering what to do when the tanker put on speed. But it was already going too fast to get off.

I hung on for several miles and then a bus came up behind and I saw the driver waving, shouting and grimacing, blowing his horn. The bus put on an unsafe spurt to pass the tanker. I despised him. *Hysterical sod, he's going to warn the tanker driver*. And he did. The tanker stopped. I hopped off and sat on the grass verge under the hedge. The driver got out, came back, and looked at me and then the tap. Mystified, he looked more closely at me and got back into the cab. Before he closed the door I was behind the tanker where he couldn't see me. The moment it started I was up on the tap again.

Miles later it slowed at a depot and I got off, passed the driver's cab on the inside and walked on without looking back. I thought of the men escaping from prisoner of war camps in Germany and tramping across Europe. Head down, inconspicuous, stoic. I smiled. We would recognize each other on the street.

At the end of the afternoon I was beat. The sole of my left shoe was holed and I felt the small sharp stones on the road. Seeing a railway station I walked up boldly, bought a penny platform ticket at the machine and went in. I walked around as if I knew where I was going until I found the platform for Liverpool and a short four-carriage train waiting there. I picked one with compartments so that I would not be caught by a ticket inspector.

I chose a small rural station to try my escape. A platform, a grass bank leading up from it and no fence. At the exit was a railwayman collecting tickets from a couple of passengers. There was no time to waste.

I sprinted up the bank hearing the shouting behind me. As always, it was "Stop him!" Over on my right was a track across a field joining a row of cottages parallel to it and ending with a gap in a hedge along the main road. I ran hard until I was abreast the cottages where men were gardening or idling about, smoking. Their heads lifted as they saw me and heard the shouts from the railwayman who was now running towards them.

Jesus, they'll nab me before I get to the hedge, I thought, putting on my best sprint, seeing nothing but the gap and traffic passing beyond it. I reached the road and, would you believe it, there was a big, white delivery truck, high and square, passing right in front of me. The rear doors were shut with a hasp and a padlock. There was a step beneath them. I jumped and grabbed the padlock, foot on the step. I twisted round to see the men burst from the hedge staring at me with a drop-jawed, 'I'll-be-damned' look on their faces, shaking their fists.

I stared back but made no rude gestures, much as I wanted to. "They may get you yet," I said. In any case I needed both hands to grip the lock as the truck accelerated.

There was no traffic following but soon there were houses and shops. The first grin came at the moment of recognition. I was in Woolton, at the end of the bus route from Liverpool. I dropped off the truck, legs pedalling in the air so I'd hit the road running to avoid falling flat on my face. I had pennies enough for the bus fare and sat back, eyes closing with sleep for the half hour journey home.

The next day in school during my fifth form French lesson, I noticed that old Edwards was staring at me suspiciously.

"Nott."

"Sir?"

"What's the rule?"

"In the perfect tense with *avoir* as auxiliary the past participle agrees in number and gender with the preceding direct object."

"Hum. Write an example on the blackboard."

I got up and limped to the front wincing as I reached up with the chalk to write, "Le gendarme les a déjà achetées'. *Les* being, in this case, the object pronoun for *les fleurs* which is feminine plural. The policeman has already bought them".

Mr. Edwards studied me as I went back to my desk.

"Well, it seems you've done your *French* homework, whatever *else* you've been doing this weekend," he said knowingly.

I considered him. Nice man, good teacher. I thought of the roaring and banging of the night, of the risks, of the total loneliness, of the helplessness if something goes wrong. *Yes, but you don't know anything, Mr. Edwards*, I thought from inside my proud, juvenile exclusivity, *and you'll never know it from me. I have an ocean of experience and a mind-set you don't have and will never hear about. I keep it to myself.* It was a thought, forever juvenile, that I'd repeat for the next thirty-one years. But always with the proviso that there were a host of men above me with far longer rough-life credentials.

Chapter 14

María

"I could see his back teeth through the cut in his face," she said. "He had slashes on his head, neck and ribs and his arms were in ribbons, all bloody. He was lying just here in the sugar-cane. Four months ago. We'd lived together for five years."

She was fighting for control. I took her arm and led her away down the dirt track through the cane. We went back to her isolated house, adobe walls, tin roof, no light, and no water. Her five-year-old daughter Carmen, was there, and her mother in the outside kitchen, three bamboo walls and a wood fire. Like thousands more in El Salvador.

"There was no money at all after they killed him," she said, "so I went across the frontier to Guatemala City where a girl from the village was working in the bar where you found me."

The bar was *Los Calzoncillos* – a notorious bordello on

a dirt road in a dark area of Zona 12, Guatemala City. Fired up by six rums in the hotel and dared by a local newsman, I went there. The noise hit me from outside in the street. Inside, four girls were doing a clumsy strip encircled by swaying, shouting men swigging beer from the bottle. Men were taking girls to the back rooms and a bouncer would bang on the door after fifteen minutes.

I noticed a girl alone on a bench and sat by her, out of the way. Her name was María and she'd been there three weeks, she said.

"It's rough but I have a little girl and a mother in El Salvador to look after."

We talked for some time. Then the light caught her face. It was Edwardian, white, level brows, lips curving down, serious sweet.

I said, "If you give this ten-dollar bill to the boss can you leave with me instead of us going to a room here?"

She stared and said, "Espera… wait." She came back with a spare shirt and pants in a plastic bag.

"Okay?" I said.

"Sí." She was flustered.

"The boss?"

"Sí, he's an animal. But I'll have to come back here when, when…"

"Yes," I said, "I guess so."

In two days at the hotel I discovered she was twenty-four, couldn't read or write, was not sure what Europe was and hadn't heard of the atom bomb. She was raw sensitive, reserved, silent. The staff were gentle with her. The woman newspaper seller on the corner said, "She's a love, señor. You take care of her, hear?"

Haltingly, she told her story. It was not the guerrillas nor the army nor the death squads who killed her husband, it was the neighbours. In the middle of the dirty war against the Marxist guerrillas the Salvadorean government in a surprise move, seized, with compensation, all holdings over 1250 acres and handed them to committees of workers. Hers was a big one with two hundred and fifty families, a sugar mill, workshops and transport.

"Plenty of work?" I asked.

"Sí, everyone had a job. But not for long."

The committee elected for six months by the workers was advised by a delegate from the Institute for Agrarian Transformation. A weakling who followed what they wanted. In a few months the mill was closed with mechanical failures, the transport cannibalized because the spare parts had been sold, and work was scarce. Under the next committee things got worse. The new members soon had electricity and television sets. They began to hand out tokens to give a day's work. Cronies and relations got them. She got only two in a month and then none.

Her husband threatened to go to the Institute. The

committee men, ordinary men, gripped by greed and facing the single chance of their lives to slake it, turned gangsters and murdered him.

That's a story and a half, I thought. "Let's go down there," I said.

The hacienda was west of the capital, San Salvador, along the double highroad divided by a concrete apron the campesinos used to dry coffee beans. There was an army camp housing the notorious Atlacatl Battalion, sort of commandos who shoot on sight. Opposite this we turned off and in three kilometres of narrow dirt road got to her house. On the way we passed a cement-block building, painted dark green, with scruffy outbuildings and a pick-up truck jacked up on blocks.

"That's the store," she said. "They gave me credit for a bit but then stopped it when I couldn't pay. There are two daughters," she said. "They went to school. I couldn't. I had to work in the cane since I was little. They look down on me."

We stayed that night. Next day I probed around alone talking to anyone I met.

"Be careful or they'll leave you in the sugar cane too," María said.

I found four committee men. Three were straws. One was a harsh, aggressive bad hat. Sly and dangerous.

Better come back tomorrow with a pass from the

Institute, I thought. But already it was a story. It would be seized on by the right-wing to reject agrarian reform and downplayed by the left. The fringe do-gooders, longing to 'reach out' to the workers, to empower them, would pretend they hadn't seen it.

"They hadn't seen the back teeth, either," I mumbled to myself as I started on the main route out then circled back to María's house.

We left for the capital, San Salvador. Along the track there were two girls walking ahead. María said, "Stop, stop. Give them a lift." She opened the widow and said, "We're going to the city, do you want a lift?" The girls looked from her to me to the car and got in without a word. "That way you'll save your bus fare," said María with contempt.

I could feel the tension. They were the girls from the store. They were going to the travel agent to see about fares to Oklahoma. I looked at them in the mirror. There was a little whiff of pending triumph. "Oklahoma," I said, "what's up there?"

They glanced at María and one said she was going to the university with a scholarship arranged through the US embassy.

"Well, bloody damned good," I said. "What will you study, teaching, Latin American literature?"

"Petroleum engineering," she said.

I slowed the car and looked round at her. I even shook

her hand. "That's terrific," I said. "You're invading a man's world and I hope you really put one over all those machos."

We talked until we reached the city and the travel agency. The girls hopped out laughing, without a glance at María. She was sunk down in her seat. Her hands were clutched tight, the knuckles white. I understood at once and with shame. I had intended to go to a down-market hotel but swerved left across the road and into the car park of the *Camino Real*.

The doorman waved us into the huge lobby. María stopped, unnerved. There was a piano bar on the left and I steered her there and sat her at a table. She looked round from under her lashes. It was happy hour and lively. Expansive men in suits and women in dresses and heels were everywhere. She watched the pianist but remained pale and drawn.

I said, "Those girls from the store will be going home soon on the bus and walking back along the track. It's nearly night." She looked at me. "But if you want we can stay here. There's a disco." I waited a moment. "Next week I have to go to Mexico. If you like we'll get you a passport and you can go too." She said nothing. "We'll leave some money for your mother," I said and waited again. "It won't be for long. You could be back here in two weeks and, look, every day I'll split my expense money with you. You save it, you can look after Carmen." She lowered her head and was moving it from side to side. Thinking I'd lost her, I ducked to look. But she was not saying no. She was smiling. The first smile since I'd known her. And as things worked out, the first of many more.

Chapter 15

Pay etc.

"But that's cocky-watchman's pay," I blurted, warmed by gin and tonic.

We were in the *Travellers Club* at 'luncheon', the contact who had been assigned for my visit to London and a senior man whose name and position were not mentioned. It was the most extraordinary thing I said in all those years, most un-MI6. The senior man looked pained, either by the expression I used or by the mere mention of money.

Alarmed, I glanced at the contact. I thought I saw a grin strangled at birth.

I had seen a piece in the *Times* reporting pay for a London policeman or a sub- lieutenant in the Navy with one year's service, higher in both cases than mine after four years. They were young sprigs of twenty-odd and I was thirty-three. I was given a raise after that meeting but it took twenty-one years before I reached 1,000 pounds a month and a local living allowance which depended on local prices. In my thirty-first and last year, my pay was 18,300 pounds a year.

If only we could tell the tax-payer, I thought, *and those grumpies in Parliament who quibbled about spending by an 'unaccountable' secret service.*

It was not only pay; expenses were rigidly controlled. At one stage during the dirty guerrilla war in Central America my case officer was based in Mexico. I would fly up when I had enough for a report, maybe after three weeks, sometimes less. This was expensive. We worked it out that it would be cheaper to buy a small car which would cut out air travel and also let me reach places difficult to get to. At the end I would sell the car and return the money. The accounts men, with slide-rules and narrowed eyes, agreed. It was more than a thousand miles to Mexico City and I drove my *VW Rabbit* up and down, delighted, fifteen times one year.

When things were rearranged I sold the car and handed over the money. Later, passing through Costa Rica, I was told I could get another one. I took a bus to Panama City where sales tax was cheaper. It took nineteen hours on a hard seat with snoring neighbours bonking their heads on mine when we went round a bend. I pictured all those suits in the City and Wall St. flying first class and raking in money while I laboured like a knight in shiny jeans to make them safe from the gulag. I didn't waste working time either. I drove seventeen hours straight to get back.

For me the perks were, firstly, total independence. You

were alone with no contact at all with a head office in case some situation needed a decision. Whatever happened you dealt with it or found your own way out. There was nowhere to run to, no one to fall back on except yourself. Also, on a lesser scale, you never clocked in to an office, never had any superior breathing down your neck, and never got into office politics or dull staff meetings. You met with a case officer at intervals and the sixteen I worked with were first class men with only one who put me through the wringer. I started with men twenty years my senior and ended with men twenty years and more my junior but all were professionals who could make their mark anywhere.

There were no pensions for agents in the field. Severance pay was a percentage of final year's salary multiplied by years of service. Of course, as I had thirty-one of those it amounted to a respectable sum.

What is harder to calculate than your status in the pay and perks league is the damage done to your nervous system, if you have one. I don't mean at all because of people shooting at you. It was more subtle and far less dramatic. It was the slow erosion of your ability to shrug off what I called the canker of lying. Jung called persistent lying a psychic poison. The dissembling, the concealment, the constant presentation of a false persona was no problem in the beginning. I was mendacious enough to like it.

The lying was based above all on my lack of cover, that crucial element in an agent's life. All I or the Firm could manage at the start was a letter from a Fleet Street flagship saying I would be contributing reporting from time to time. At best this made me a stringer. It didn't last long. New editors took over and when I tried to renew my stringership their foreign desks wrote, 'we do not need your services'.

I was never able to discover if this was because they suspected me. It would have cost them nothing to renew and might have got them a story from a trouble spot where there were no newsmen.

I wrote about petroleum in Venezuela for the Economist Intelligence Unit and contributed to the first class 'Review' of the Bank of London and South America. The curious psychological effect was to give me an unfounded confidence, or plain cheek, to print cards saying I ran an outfit called *BRITNEWS* and register it with a cable address. I couldn't go so far as to put those estimable publications on it but just the existence of the link was a boost.

I got a front page by-line in the *Observer* once and a congratulatory telegram from the foreign desk for 'fast, elegant coverage'. But it took no less than President Kennedy's and Jackie Kennedy's visit to Venezuela to get it. A news story as big as this is normally covered by staffers in the press plane landing ahead of the VIP. I got one by-line in the flagship in early days on the 'invasion' of Anguilla and did a broadcast for the *BBC* on a Law of the Sea Conference in Caracas in 1974. These were straightforward reporting.

They had no idea what I was at.

In any case, even if I'd had a connection with a newspaper, there was no day to day market for coverage from the countries I was working in. Over time it became a severe nervous drain to request a meeting with any source a third and fourth time knowing there had never been a cutting to show for the one before and very aware that I'd have nothing to show for the fifth visit either. If you add to this the constant scare that they, at least officials in government, only had to ask their embassies and you'd be exposed, or burned, as the phrase goes.

It happened in Guyana. There was trouble on the frontier in the south, the Rupununi, disputed with Venezuela. It came at just the moment the Firm wanted a look at something else there. I flew to Georgetown thinking to get down south and then offer the story to the *Times*. Confident that they would welcome an on-the-spot report from so remote a region, I told the authorities I was representing that paper. Wilier than most they got their office in London to check. The *Times* disowned me and I was told to leave the country. In other countries I was operating in I'd get far worse than being booted out.

Claiming to be a newsman or writer to get to a target

was also very necessary to getting the stuff out. I would see a dozen contacts, sometimes twenty, very few of whom had anything to offer on what I was after. I would make a normal newsman's notes, name, date and content of the interview. These were harmless for the most part but would hopefully cover what I was doing if picked up. In no case could an agent record anything at all on meetings with subversives. He kept it in his head. In my case for many years there were no clandestine meetings with case officers in the countries I was working in because he was somewhere else. I could not write a report until I left the country and only one day or night away from seeing him.

Suppose you were in a traffic accident and the police went through your bag? Suppose they caught sight of the name of a military officer or right-wing figure or guerrilla in your papers and pointed it out to their captain? Suppose he handed it to security or the secret police? Suppose you were suspected anyway and those police searched your hotel room? Suppose also that they fell into subversives' hands?

The approach to and handling of real targets like the radical wings of the communist parties including guerrillas, had an added ingredient. You had to keep your personal reactions out of it. I despised Stalinists as much as the oppressive elites. The first sent their men to murder a US ambassador, two US military attachés, and a German ambassador in Guatemala. They used kidnappings and disappearances as did the right-wing death squads. The elites encouraged their armies to murder thousands there and in El Salvador. I felt no compunction about worming in to both sides.

I wished it had been possible to get alongside some adversaries. I had always admired Richard Sorge who worked for the Soviets as a German correspondent in Tokyo. It was his tremendous intelligence work that told Moscow that Japanese forces would not invade. This allowed the Russians to move troops west to meet the German invasion.

He was a grand fellow, far and away in a higher and more dangerous league than me. Drunk as a lord, he would manoeuvre his motorbike around Tokyo to meet his contacts. Japanese secret police got him, tortured and hanged him.

In Caracas three top Communist Party leaders were jailed in the San Carlos barracks in 1964. A Syrian communist agent, Nehemet Chagin, alias Simon, twenty-eight, rented a scruffy little grocer's shop opposite the prison. He made friends with the guards, puzzled out where the fugitives' cell was in relation to his shop and started tunnelling under the street.

After three years in jail the three got out. I was told by a contact in the Party to wait under the clock in the quad of the Central University at noon. A car drew up driven by a cool red-head. She told me to put on a pair of sun-glasses covered with black tape. I could see nothing. She drove every which way and out into the country, before several pairs of hands pulled me out of the car, and led me to a room in a house with a blanket over a doorway. They guided my hands to this and pushed me in.

"You can take the glasses off now," someone said.

In a cloud of cigarette smoke were the three fugitives, Teodoro Petkoff, Pompeyo Márquez, and Guillermo Garcìa Ponce. The whole army and police were scouring the country for them. They gave me the usual revolutionary stuff about the oppressed people (quite right), and the greedy elite (right again). I did a story for *United Press International* and so fulfilled my part of the bargain: publicity. Simon got back to Damascus safe and sound. He and Sorge were what the North West Frontier colonel would call 'dashed sporting chaps'.

In the 70's I wrote two adventure books and two novels. They were published in English, French, Spanish and Japanese. At times I tried to use this as cover but it was curiously ineffective. After this added failure to find cover I was beginning to ask myself where the fun had gone, the little swagger after having pulled off a particularly adroit trick.

Then I read in a volumn of Browning, in a reference to Sludge the Medium: 'And now and again in his course of fraud did he not turn a wistful eye towards any reckless tatterdemalion, if only the vagrant lived in freedom and truth'. For me for so many years the tatterdemalion could be any untrained, struggling stringer so long as he had 'truth' – that accreditation in his pocket that I so badly lacked.

On a plane from New York I talked with a passenger of about my age who was an accountant with an international firm, who was flying to Rio to do a requested audit of a company's books. He would be met at the airport and taken to a hotel. The company would welcome him and do everything possible to help. They wanted him. I'd never thought the word wistful could have any meaning in my life but I understood it then. I'd make do without someone at the airport with my name on a placard and a car outside. But what wouldn't I give to be authentic, to find an open door instead of sneaking in the back way, to get on with a job without acting out a lie, without watching like a hawk for the slightest wariness on my target's face.

If my movements coincided with a big story I had to avoid the hotel where the foreign press was lodged and stay away from the bar where they gathered. What to say when I was inevitably asked which paper I was from? I had the constant image of my saying 'the *Telegraph*' or whatever and a reporter in the group saying, 'that's strange because so am I'.

A case officer in later years once said, with organizational satisfaction, while we talked over a coming assignment that needed special caution,

"Well, you're a well-known writer in Central America so…"

He was so far off reality that I didn't reply. First, no one who hasn't been a newsman would know what it's about. Second, if I explained it he might alert London. I wanted no such fuss. They might even pull me out. I preferred to go on in my 'course of fraud' even though it was wearing me down. As one author put it: 'Your job is the loneliest and most thankless in the world'. I was jauntily pleased it was so, in the beginning.

Chapter 16

Atlantic

A Great White shark charged our plywood boat at astonishing speed. Surely it was going to ram us? We stumbled to the mast and clung to the shrouds. Its big curving fin stuck up out of the water. We could see its grey back and mottled sides. Just as it reached the bow it went under, turned over about ten feet down and flashed underneath showing its white belly as wide as a pick-up. Its big fin shot up out of the water on the other side of the boat as it turned upright and hurtled away. At about seventy yards distance it wheeled and came at us again. At the bow it did the same trick. About the fourth time we were able to speak. Anneke mumbled about going below to get her camera.

"Don't you move," I said. I surmised hopefully that it was a male putting it on for the boat which was white too and nine feet wide, about his size. I didn't want to think of him trying to couple. After about fifteen minutes it shot away to starboard and vanished. We were two days east and maybe 220 miles from the nearest land, the island of Antigua. My log entry says it looked twenty feet long, ten feet less than the boat.

We'd had our tight little moments before on this voyage from Plymouth to Tenerife and the West Indies. Only three days and two hundred and sixty miles out, course 220 magnetic, the boat had been tearing through the night, down one wave into the trough and up the next, corkscrewing in the foam, with a howling north to nor' nor' west gale behind her. We'd heard the broadcast gale warning to ships off Finisterre, rigged the storm sail alongside the jib and reefed the mainsail. I thought that sounded real salty but I hadn't a clue except for what I'd read in the ocean sailing manuals.

Now, nine at night, great black waves glinting in the moonlight, spume running down their huge slopes, the rigging whistling, and water thumping into the cockpit, I saw the speed log needle jammed against the 11 knots mark in a boat with a hull speed of six. I thought we'd trip up and flip over or dive under. Idiot, I tried to hand haul the mainsail down to double reef but tore it at two reef ties.

Clinging on to the tiller in a foot and a half of water, watching the masthead scrawling figures of eight against the stars, I recalled the mantra: 'In a gale, heave to and ride it out'. I pulled the tiller up to my chest and we swung round to starboard, heeled way over to port, with me thinking, *Is this when we get capsized and sink?* She came into the wind at last, sails cracking like gunshots. I kept the main amidships and the tiller up while Viv winched the jib sheet tight to hold the boat. Hove to, we'd be steady and riding up the waves but the jib overcame the opposing rudder, the mainsail took up and we started off nor' nor' west at three knots just off the wind. At this rate we'd end in Newfoundland instead of the Canaries if the boat held out against big waves thumping into the starboard bow.

"Viv," I shouted, "we should run with it. But we'll have to come about." Like, go back the way we came.

"Come about?" Viv yelled. "In a gale?" He'd read the manual too.

What we feared was broaching, what the show-off sailors call the death roll. It means that when you come broadside to the wind it can capsize you especially if it's gale force and being helped to tip you by big waves running in the same direction and pushing. Well, here goes. I put the tiller down and we turned to port where the jib filled tight. Again the wind caught us beam-on and we heeled until the scuppers were under water.

Going round, I watched the mainsail, Viv on the sheet trying to get it filled slowly without slamming into the shrouds. But it did. He got the sheet on the winch and hauled it off the shrouds tight as a drum. He slacked off the jib until it steadied.

We yelled in triumph as the boat stood upright and

surged on. In a few moments we realized *Lady Milly* was behaving just as she was before I got het up about her speed, before we got to remembering mantras that didn't apply, and before we got to heaving to and coming about again. All for nothing. But we would not forget how a boat feels when it's trimmed right for course and wind. We'd come through, learned a lesson and felt like sailors. We waited for applause from the rest of the crew, but down below in their bunks the girls slept right through it.

They were Pippa, daughter of the last captain of the *Ark Royal* and Anneke, a friend of Viv, both of whom were eighteen. I was the old geezer at fifty. I had never considered a crew. Not because I was a bold solo sailor, but because my only experience had been in a twenty-one-footer off the coast of Venezuela and a first-time ocean skipper has no business taking inexperienced young 'uns aboard for an Atlantic crossing. I fretted far more about that than about the voyage, but Viv was fired up and would have been outraged to be left behind after so much work re-rigging the boat, buying sails, and making forays into the Channel. Pippa turned up with her sea-bag at the last moment. At least she'd been to sea in schooners.

The boat was a thirty-one-foot Golden Hind sloop called Ishtar. I changed that for *Lady Milly* after my daughter. It was slow in mild weather, strong and steady in rough. While fitting her out I took a five-day celestial navigation course with a merchant marine captain working with the

University of Southampton. We slogged through the traditional steps, with diagrams of the earth sphere with slices cut out and lines going from the centre to the celestial sphere, mucho geometry and abstruse vocabulary. The real problem being, as always, that shooting sun sights onshore is a far cry from doing it against the heave and roll of a small boat at sea.

A sextant is a lovely thing and as demanding as sighting from a running jeep on a moving target with a rifle at eight hundred yards. It's a shame it has been ousted in the world's great navies by the satellite gizmo you can hold in your hand or carry in your car. There was no GPS when we made the crossing. I sat on the cabin roof, one foot on the guard rail, my watch on the inside of my left wrist. You bring the sun down near to the horizon and hold your head and eye steady while you swing the instrument like a pendulum. When the sun just touches the horizon at the bottom of the arc of the pendulum you get it precise as you can with a vernier screw and note the time. I'd have a notebook under my rear-end and a pencil in my teeth.

In fine old style you should shout 'mark' and a crewman watching the ship's chronometer down below would note the time. Our chronometer was so beautiful and brassy on the varnished bulkhead I thought it was just an ornament for a previous day-sailing owner. My wristwatch was a low-price *Casio* which I would correct by signals on a Russian shortwave radio four times as big and heavy as the ones in the suave yachting shops but which, at 22 pounds sterling, was the cheapest on the market. My sextant was East German: of stark design, and marvellously machined, in a well-carpentered wooden box. The Firm would have looked askance at doing business with 'Them'.

Getting the sight is the hardest part. The sun would jerk all over the place, waves would get higher than your head and hide it, and spray would slap you in the face. You had to get it in an instant.

It was best to take three shots. I'd take five sometimes when we were really jumping around. Then down below, one hand for the sextant, one for the boat, put it carefully into its box and stow it. The working of the sight takes twenty-two calculations and running your finger down tables in three volumes. An idea of its magic is that you are sighting the sun ninety-three million miles away and to avoid inaccuracy you have to enter your height of eye off the sea. In *Lady Milly* this was about seven feet.

Viv and the girls demanded lessons. There was a plastic sextant aboard in case we lost the good one. I had a chance here to put an old instinct to work; drop the theory. Just do it.

I said not a word about azimuths, celestial spheres and equinoxes. I just showed them how to handle the sextant. When they got this we went through the tables. Twenty-two steps. Then how to plot it on the position-line chart. It took twenty-four days from Tenerife to Antigua and they were all navigating by the time we were halfway across.

By November 30 we were two thousand miles out from Plymouth on a balmy day. We slacked off sails and two by two went over the stern and fell behind on a thirty-foot rope. We could feel the gentle tug of the boat. I thought there was more of a tug from several miles of water beneath us. If the day was balmy we were stark mad.

Apart from our playful Great White, dolphins were often with us and flying fish were skittering across the surface. In a snooty yachting shop a young salesman had told us with great authority that we'd need a weighted line to get fish. We bought it, trawled it and got nothing in thirty-nine days at sea.

The day after our encounter with the shark, at dawn, the boom broke in two. First, I was trying to get a sight on Venus, which we didn't need but which kept my eyes off the deck. Second, we had no fore-guy rigged. Third, the wind was creeping round south of east and got behind the sail. Fourth, the boom held by it's kicking-strap, which should have kept it from swinging up was made of un-elastic rope and was taut straight down to the deck. Most of the boom's length doubled back against the mast like some ancient yardarm. I jumped below, stowed the sextant and yelled to the others. We all erupted on deck to view the disaster.

"Right, you lot," said Pippa, brightly. "I'll get the tea made."

It was a lovely dawn. We knew we were only a day and a night or so out of Antigua.

Viv and I got the boom off and tied on deck. We rolled up the foot of the sail and tied it at the deep reef line. Two mornings later I came up on deck and the three crew peered at me with what I thought at first was a smirk. Then they pointed over the bow. There directly ahead was Cape Shirley and the rocky entrance to English Harbour. We were even on line for the deeper, safe channel on the right. Nearly six weeks at sea, 2,815 sea miles from Plymouth and we were dead on. As a first time navigator, it was my turn to smirk.

Viv and the girls left here to crew on bigger boats and with the boom fixed I sailed out on December 30 for Jamaica. It took seven days in the bumpy Caribbean where waves are lower and sharper than on the Atlantic. There was a twenty-four-hour storm on New Year's Day with radio warnings to small craft from St. Croix and Puerto Rico to return to port. There was no port for me except six days ahead in Port Royal. *Lady Milly* thumped through it all. I tied up at the jetty at Port Royal and climbed out of the boat. I was back on the job, two years looking for Fidel Castro's infiltrators.

The Atlantic can be savage but it was the Pacific where I almost got my throat cut...

With dictator Somoza ousted by socialist–Marxist rebels in Nicaragua and dirty guerrilla wars in Guatemala and El Salvador, 1980 saw me taking the boat through the Panama Canal and up the Pacific to berth in Acapulco, while I worked in those stricken countries for the next ten years.

My old editor Dennis Fawcett came down for the sail to Panama City and a friend, Mark Jefferson, asked to be dropped in Punta Arenas, Costa Rica, to return to his forestry work in Jamaica. When they'd gone I made a few repairs and was ready to leave when a launch drew alongside and John, a big, strapping lady-killer-hunk young American asked if he could crew up as far as I was going. He said he had small boat experience – turned out to be on motor boats – and I said come aboard.

On the long sail down the bay into the open sea he said he belonged to a cult which believed they were reincarnations and were destined to live their previous experiences over again in their present lives. He handed me the book of doctrine and urged me to read it. I should have.

We had headwinds all down the bay and rounded Cabo Blanco in the dark. The navigating light was not working which meant that neither it nor the Nicoya Gulf main entrance light was showing. Typical, we huffed. As soon as we turned the expected port beam winds failed too.

A good six hundred and forty miles on we reached Mexico where the motor seized while we were becalmed in the Gulf of Tehuantepec and we were being rolled ashore by lazy pushful waves. Nearby was a commercial fishing boat with the same trouble. They shouted that their propeller was fouled by a cable and could we help. We had snorkels and wire cutters and bargained that we'd fix them if they would then tow us back to a fishing hell-hole for repairs with some money and my Greek sailor cap thrown in. John grabbed his tools, dived in and very quickly cut away the cable. He promptly secured it to their stern and brought the other end back to us. His size assured there was no objection. We were towed in and a mechanic called El Gato, because he had yellow eyes, simply drained water from our engine and we were off.

There was little wind and becoming more grumpy by the hour we steered dully across the huge bay. Our electric Tillermaster was not working and it was tiller, sleep, tiller, sleep. I learned that out of the trade winds this apparatus would be a godsend. Throughout all these trials John had become a devoted fisherman. He would float a lure astern and quickly haul in five-pounders we couldn't name. It was so fertile he would throw back anything that looked the wrong size for the pan, or was not plump enough. I told him we didn't have to massacre a school of fish for breakfast.

The small cockpit was smeared in blood and the clacking of our nine-inch gutting knife, honed down on the cutting board to a razor-sharp blade half its original width, was getting tedious.

A day or two beyond the bay, both of us in the cockpit, knees touching, John bloodily slicing, me coaxing the tiller to keep the wind in the sails, I felt something was off. John was fidgeting, muttering, distraught. Suddenly he jerked forward, his face inches from mine.

"I know you, Dave; we were on a big three-master rounding the Horn and I killed you, Dave, for a lousy two dollars you hid in your hammock."

"With a marlin spike, John?"

"With a knife, Dave," he said, whipping up that vicious blade with its point at my throat.

I looked up at the sail, sort of routine. "If you go ahead and kill me again you can't navigate, you can't sail. You'll drift out southwest where there's nothing."

The knife was still there. His eyes, staring, didn't blink.

"You'll run out of food. You'll run out of water and you'll die madder than you are now," I said.

His eyes widened, perhaps at the sheer insolence of what I had said.

After a long minute he put the knife down. "Ah, forget it, Dave," he said, beginning to tidy up.

We were three days from port, miles offshore. I didn't sleep much. When we tied up in Acapulco I was dead beat and stretched out on my bunk. John, bright as a starling, pulled a russet suit from his bag to go with his green eyes and made for the *Princess Hotel* in an obviously well practiced predatory manoeuvre.

I discovered later my credit card went with him.

David, Milly and papa off Portsmouth, 1978

In the Panama Canal, moving the boat from Jamaica to California to sell her, 1980.

Lone, steady crewmate crossing to Jamaica - the wind vane, steering the ship

Mid-Atlantic at its quietest so a dip in the ocean on the end of a rope. Idiots.

Sail trials off Portsmouth before the ocean crossing. I had not yet painted out her original name, Ishtar, for Lady Milly, my daughter, October 1978

Viv securing rolled up mainsail after boom broke 220 miles from Antigua after 38 days at sea

Chapter 17

Gizmos

The microphone was set in one of my cufflinks. This was before the electronics' era. The wire went up my sleeve and down to a recorder tucked in the waistband of my trousers. Being a shorty and thin this meant I had to keep my jacket on. By the way, all talk of fellows with a Browning 9mm in a shoulder holster or tucked in their belt fore or aft and not letting it show only goes for big, beefy chaps in loose clothes. The recorder, small as it was, would have stuck out of my skinny waistline. Keeping my jacket on meant sweating. The restaurant was hot, the booth more so. The Argentine mixed grill on the charcoal burner alongside the table was crackling. My companion, tie and coat off, biting into his garlic bread said (what else):

"Don't you feel the heat?"

I did but I wanted to get it across to London who'd sent this gizmo in the diplomatic pouch to try out. The techno wizards would replay it in their workshop. I fought to resist saying I was keeping my coat on because I was bleeding from a stab wound in the heart but didn't want a fuss. I had to make the point about heat. I said, deadpan, that I was practicing for a formal dinner down on the coast in an old mansion that still had only fans on the ceiling to move the hot air around a bit.

"You know how the Caracas rich are when entertaining in their beach palaces," I said.

He'd never been in one but nodded his head sagely. He was the guinea pig. I hardly knew him. In no way would I have made such a trial with a contact.

We had not much to talk about in fact until he said he was a cross-country motorbike fan. Me too. My bike was a Spanish *Ossa*, which I thought was classy. I told him I'd gone to the practice ground south of the city where there was a steep, 200-foot, dirt and stone slope for controlled descents. I had wanted to do one of those take-off jumps over the edge, not a cautious front wheel first and ease the bike over manoeuvre. I had twitched the throttle, taken off in the air, landed down the slope far too fast, grabbed the brakes, and catapulted over the rightwards-pointing wheel with a leg jammed between the petrol tank and the handlebar.

The bike and I took it in turns vaulting over each other until we came apart and slid to a stop. This was the ninth of ten fractures I'd been fool enough to invite, and the worst. A spiral with splinters. I couldn't move and had difficulty enough not sliding down further. It was a weekday. There was none of the crowd of aficionados practicing on weekends. I shouted and gave out my famous sheep herders' taxi whistle. Nothing. There was no house nearby and only a dirt road going nowhere. After an hour down in the dumps I heard a bike. Lady Luck prompted the rider to stop his engine on the flat ground above the slope. I whistled again. He peered over and slid down. He was young, out there after school. He was alone. I couldn't have got up the slope even if he had someone with him. It was beginning to dawn on me that I was in a mess. He looked at my bike, my leg, and then up and down the slope. And with sudden authority said, "Wait."

After another hour the boy and two toughs in firemen's work clothes, slid down the slope with a wooden board with slots for handholds. One got my boot off and pulled a tight elastic net like a sock up over the fracture, saying 'okay, okay' when I yipped. They tied me to the board, got me up the slope and down to a truck and to the clinic. One gave me a hand to grip en route. They were first class. The boy too. The next day, with me still in the clinic, he returned the *Ossa* to where I lived without leaving his name.

A month later I left a letter at the small fire station on the outskirts where they worked. It said I had had the great pleasure of recounting the event to an assembly of fire service officers in England who applauded the work of their Venezuelan colleagues. They were very pleased and put it on the bulletin-board. They deserved every word of it. Of course, I didn't know any fire officers and had not been to England.

My dinner partner said, seriously, "Didn't you know you don't ever go out moto-crossing alone?" I took this well-deserved rebuke and looked at him with more interest.

"Who did you send the letter to?" he said.

"The station chief. He was a captain."

"That's the trouble with these firemen," he said with some venom. "They use military ranks and insignia they have no right to."

"Why are you so peeved about it?" I asked.

"I'm an army officer, a lieutenant."

I twitched my cuff.

He had been operating against the guerrillas in the mountainous area to the east. These operations were not being broadcast by the government. He said his patrol had shot a guerrilla below them in a steep ravine. The body lay on a flat rock where the stream went over in a waterfall.

"We knew they'd come back for him. We took aim and waited. Not a word or movement. We were there the whole day till dusk. A man ran across the rock and grabbed the body. We shot him."

Later, I handed the gizmo to my case officer with a sly grin.

"They'll like that," I said.

Like it? There wasn't a word on it.

Some years later I needed another kind of gizmo. There was a drive on to get business for Britain as well as uncover Reds. Where better than Venezuela? The country was rich in resources. It was the world's biggest oil exporter. It had huge mountains of iron ore and bauxite, coalfields and wide hydro power potential in its rivers. It already had giant generators at the Guri Dam and a steel mill. But the Brits had missed out on contracts. We knew there was new planning on a grand scale.

I probed at a fairly high level and got nowhere. These contacts were not in on it. There had to be a windowless room somewhere where it all was being hatched. My case officer said we had to get into the spot where the ideas slipped into the planners' heads, before they'd even done a sketch on their scratchpads and then listen out for echoes in the development, public works and finance offices. Nada. These guys were members of a very exclusive club of technologists. They did not see themselves this way, of course. They were not moving around in dark glasses but were telling no one except themselves what they were doing especially not their ministerial bosses who didn't know a spanner from a wrench. I began to view industrial espionage with respect.

Getting nowhere in the capital I went down to Puerto Ordaz where the Caroní River joins the Orinoco. It is the hub of the steel, iron, and aluminium enterprises. The oil boom was in full flood. The government was 'sowing the petrodollar' like confetti. One plant manager I saw waved through the window at a parking lot of 1,200 trailers, home to as many or more foreign industrial experts. Many wiser Venezuelans called this the 'sheik mentality' meaning 'we don't need to produce technicians, these fellows can be hired'. I got in to talk to several high-ups. They were working full out, so much so I was embarrassed to take up their time. In any case I got nothing out of it.

This left Maracaibo, in the far west, in a major oil field. I flew up there with not much enthusiasm. Delving into planning was almost as slow as infiltrating a commie cell. In this hot and sticky city I was able to track down the local equivalent of the windowless room. Not only that but also the coordinator, a young man with reddish-hair, and glasses. I'd put him down as a postgrad doctoral candidate at a northern Brit university. He invited me from his poky office to a modest bistro for a coffee. By the way, no one in the world makes a cup of coffee better than the Venezuelans, any of them, from a lad in the street who pours it out of a thermos tank on his back into a paper cup to a swish restaurant. We sipped our brew and I spun my line.

He took me into a back room in the office. He pointed to a shelf with thirteen two-inch thick, full-size binders.

"It's all in there," he said. "I'll leave you to look at it. Take your time."

Wide-eyed, I pulled down the first one. The index.

Blast furnaces, coke plants, coal mining and an astonishing sort of aqueduct-slide to bring down the coal twenty miles in a slurry. All to feed a steel complex fed with iron ore shipped down the Orinoco and along the coast to docks yet to be built. Roads, railways, all the myriad controls and electrics to be installed. I opened the binder for the blast furnaces. Pages and pages of specifications. I opened another.

The same.

What I saw too clearly was the billions of money that would go into this. There must be a chance for a hundred foreign companies to rush in and thrive. It had filtered in from London that Brit businessmen were being left at the post by the Americans, the Germans, the Swiss and the Japanese, worldwide. It even occurred to me that I could tote a copy round the UK and earn a million in commission. I'd gladly do it for free and for the Queen, of course. I stood aghast in that office. My pulse was hammering in my ears. 'What is to be done?' as Lenin asked. I knew damn well. I should have had a gizmo. A fiendish little camera with a roll for a thousand shots and a battery for a thousand flashes. I could have done the job in fifty minutes, say an hour. But all I had was a pocket notebook and a ballpoint pen.

Examining recorder that didn't...

Chapter 18

Golden Girl

She was small, dark-honey with the ruddy cheeks of the highland Maya Indian, vivid in her brocaded blouse, and meek as she brought in the big soup tureen from the kitchen to the serving table. A warm, glowing little presence in the sombre, panelled dining room.

Across the table was the host I'd dubbed the Duke of Devonshire of Guatemala, for his land holdings, and his patrician style. I'd had only a glimpse from behind at her glossy black hair as she had left his library before dinner, leaving the tray with whiskey and ice next to our chairs. But I hadn't missed her acute nervousness and her timorous, tiny steps beneath the long skirt of the Keq'chi women. Now I watched her circling the table with her tray for each guest to serve himself. I could see it was heavy and when it was my turn I heard her quick breathing. I had never felt anxiety vibrations like it. Tremulous in case she made a mistake in turning the tray so each serving bowl came in front of the guests as they helped themselves, she looked at no one. She was a lone, vulnerable waif alien to all in the room.

I thought of mine host's ancient Spanish family name and his Harvard-trained lawyer's precision, as he talked of helicoptering down to his farms on the Pacific coast, and what a blessing to be free of muddy landing strips. I bet he had not even noticed this girl was in his house, a new addition since the last time I was there. She put a small silver jug of hot water in front of me. I poured a little coffee from a small glass flask into a tiny cup and added the water as she passed on to my host. He was explaining how the concentrated coffee was distilled by a lifelong servant too old for any other work, filtering it slowly through a porous *tinaco*, an earthen bowl even older than she was. I watched the girl again as she left, almost fled, the dining room.

In the next few days I made the thousand-mile drive to Mexico City to see two hidden Guatemalan exiles and my case officer. In the city centre, the zona viva, I paused at a street vendor's tray filled with decidedly pretty enamelled silver bracelets. There was a shiny black number with inlaid white flowers and green vines. Of a sudden I recalled the anxious face of the servant girl and wondered how it would change if this pretty bauble was her own to keep.

Back in Guatemala I drove to my host's old house. My mind ran fast as I knocked, fingering the bracelet in my pocket. I'll catch her as soon as she opens the door. I'll only have a dangerous second. I'll just put it in her hand and shush her to silence. I can't lurk there for an instant longer. The shame I would feel if I was caught committing such a heinous breach of behaviour made me cringe.

The wide, wooden door opened and there stood my host. The Duke opening the door? He saw the surprise on my face and explained that there was a birthday party for his youngest daughter, twelve. In the crowded reception room she came up to greet me, her face alive with party joy. What could I do? I put my hand in my pocket.

"Never let it be said," I said, "that I forget the birthdays of the lovely daughters of my friends. Here," I said, taking her hand and slipping the bracelet onto her wrist.

"Why, Don David, how could you have known?" she said, whirling into the crowd to show it off.

The golden one was not there. I never saw her again.

Don't write it, just whisper. Curacao 1969.

Chapter 19

Secret Police

"Don't shout. Don't struggle. Get in the car."

The voice was level, quiet, menacing. I was standing on the pavement in front of a rent-apartment-hotel on 11th Street, Zone 1, Guatemala City. I had signed in at reception, taken my bag up to my room and had come down again to park the car.

It was Sunday. No one was in the street.

"Get in," he said.

He was tall, thin, hatchet faced. Dark shades, blue wind-jacket, black trousers and boots. I knew it immediately. DIT. Guatemala's Gestapo.

"Estás loco," I said, "you're crazy."

He stepped in close. "I've got a man across the street. Don't resist. Get in the car."

He gestured with his right hand in his jacket pocket. It stuck out too far in front to be his finger. It was his gun.

I slammed the car door shut and retreated across the

pavement. He shoved me against the wall of the hotel with his left hand and raised his gun hand pointing at my chest, his face working in rage.

"Get in the car or I'll kill you."

I spun to my right urgently recalling training. If he's got a gun stuck in your ribs you can turn fast before he gets off his first shot, they say. Before he fires again you're supposed to back into him, get your arm over his gun arm, grab his gun hand with your left and fight him. Instead I fled through the door, ran to the fire stairs and was up to the fourth floor in seconds.

I had just arrived from Mexico City, a thousand miles north, where after a week's search I'd located a Guatemalan guerrilla hideout. It was a back room in a tenement and my contact was crouched over what looked like a rudimentary ham-radio with the antenna hooked up outside the window.

I felt sorry for him right away, in this scruffy room, knowing no one.

I put my hand on his shoulder. "Don't get up," I said. "I don't want to interrupt."

"I can't connect anyway," he said, dropping his earphones on the table. I looked around.

"What's up?" I said. "The Salvadoreans have a big office."

"I'm with ORPA." This was the newest and smallest of the four guerrilla groups in

Guatemala, before Castro demanded they unite as

URNG. "We haven't got ourselves set up yet," he said, defensively.

We talked and gradually, with my standard line as anti-elite, anti-land owner, anti- oppression, but not communist, he relaxed. Relaxed enough to give me a letter for an underground colleague planted in Guatemala City. He would never in a million years have done this if he could get through on his radio. He also gave me a printed fifty page analysis of the fight for social justice in Central America. This proved academic with no serious intelligence in it.

Driving south out of Mexico City, through the rolling, pine-clad hills, Popocatepetl and its snows on the right, I sang triumphantly. The letter was under the flap at the bottom of my bag which had never been discovered by customs anywhere. It wasn't a product of the tricks department of MI6. I'd bought it in a luggage shop in Caracas. I was going to get into the guerrillas, find out their weapons and supply lines, numbers, contact with the Nicaraguan Marxists, and any direct contact with Cuba. It was a real stroke of luck. But about five hundred miles closer to the frontier I began to get the willies.

What if I was searched and they found the letter? Dead agents are no use.

Going through Tapachula and almost at the border I stopped the car where the only things in sight were six big vultures ripping at something on the road. It was a five-foot snake, eyes gone, belly opened. This lonely stretch of road ran through cane fields, high and dense. I took the pamphlet out of my bag and threw it as far as I could. I knew I'd run into an army roadblock once into Guatemala.

But when it came to the letter I just could not do it. It was too much of a prize.

Five miles later across the border, there it was. The first roadblock. I stopped, got out of the car and greeted the soldiers warmly, saluting the sergeant a little further up the road with the main patrol.

"Open the bag," they said.

I opened the rear hatch of my car, boldly unzipped the bag, pulled the top layer of clothes aside and gestured 'there-you-go', to the squaddies. They, barely literate youths, delved curiously into it. They pushed their hands down inside getting very close to the flap.

Then one of them saw on the floor the folding, reflector triangle to warn traffic if your car is stalled. He turned it over in his hands. He couldn't make it out. He looked at his mate who pulled his slung carbine to his front and called the sergeant. In this army you couldn't tell who were the killers, the mass-murderers or the normal soldiers. The sergeant walked up. He was stocky, grey-haired, leathery. He listened to the two soldiers and shook his head sadly, paternally, and told them what it was.

"Disculpe, señor, sorry sir, they don't know anything

about anything I'm afraid," he said waving me through. I sang along with the radio's plangent ranchero music all the way to Guatemala City. And now this. DIT.

I raced along the corridor to my room, threw the bag on the bed, tipped everything out, lifted the secret flap and pulled out the letter. In the bathroom I ripped it in pieces and flushed it down the loo. But here's one of those facts of life you don't know until you try. About half the paper went down. The rest, with the writing quite clear, floated there.

Expecting a hammering on the door any minute, I lifted the tank top, saw that the cistern was still empty, grabbed the scraps of paper and chewed them.

The telephone rang. The man on the desk, a bit of a joker I knew well, said in a tight, scared voice, "This is reception, señor; I think you'd better come down."

"Who's there? What's the problem?"

"Just get down here, please." His voice was more formal still. Trouble.

I pulled myself together on the way down and walked over to reception. I glanced outside and saw a military truck parked with a couple of bad hats leaning against it. Hundreds in the Guatemalan opposition, trades union leaders, priests, students, had seen this in their last moments before being disappeared or left on the roadside with a bullet in the head.

I turned to the two men standing by the desk. With no expression one of them said,

"A driver on the corner taxi rank phoned to say there's been a hold-up here. Describe what happened."

I told him in detail, and I hoped, like a shocked citizen.

"Describe the man."

"Well, he had black boots, dark trousers…"

Here I faltered. I realized that I was describing him and his mate. I decided to shut up about the blue wind-breaker and the shades, because that's what they both were wearing. They were Gestapo too. The silence went on for some time. Then he made some notes on his clipboard and said they'd make several turns round the block and come back if they found anything. The tone was dismissive.

If I'm lucky, that's the end of it, I thought.

But after two thousand miles driving and a week's search my preciousletter was gone.

Down the loo.

Out of the cold in Costa Rica writing up a visit to the guerilla wars up north, daughter Carina correcting spelling

Chapter 20

Lonely Woman

Wanted: commando officer type.
One night's work.
Ten pounds. Legal.

It was in the personal column of the *Daily Telegraph*. I wrote and got an answer.

I could meet the person, a woman, under the clock in Victoria Station. I said I'd have the *Financial Times* under my arm. The FT is printed on pink paper, an easy mark.

"Mr. Nott?"

She was about forty, trim, tweed skirt and jacket, stockings and modest heels, dark hair neat, but not groomed, her face serious and authoritative. We went into the cafeteria and sat at a table.

She began without preamble and loudly,

"My doctor thinks I'm mad."

I managed not to look around at gaping clients.

"A man comes over the wall from the field. He watches my windows. He runs across the roof. What I want is for him to be frightened off for good."

"You live alone?"

"With my son. He's eleven."

"You've told the police?"

"They'd scoff. They wouldn't take me seriously."

"So you want me to be on watch for a night on the chance that he'll pick that night too?"

"It's a rare night that he doesn't come." I thought for a moment. *It doesn't ring altogether true. But it could be. Anyway, it's a jaunt.*

"I'll come on Saturday. On an afternoon train."

"I have nosy neighbours. You must be discreet when you arrive. Can you think of something?"

"I will come as a grocer's deliveryman," I said. "By the way, can you get about two pounds of sand and one of your son's knee-high school socks?"

That Saturday I took a train carrying an old-fashioned brown-paper carrier bag. At the bottom of it were a cabbage, a cauliflower, and spring onions, with a girlfriend's long, white, painting smock. At the arrival station I went into the men's loo, put my jacket at the bottom of the bag, the vegetables on top and put on the smock. Following my lady client's directions, I left the station, walked three blocks down the High Street and then turned left on a curving lane to a row of whitewashed cottages with steep, red-tiled roofs.

I knocked at her door, shouted, "Grocer," and stepped inside. A huge, roaring, German Shepherd knocked me back against the door. I snatched the cauliflower by its stem and waggled it fatuously in its great jaws. I knew I was done for. Then a cheerful, definitely non-terrified small boy ran in from the back ordered the dog off with one word and motioned it to return to the cow's thigh bone it had been splintering on the floor.

"The dog will behave now," said a quiet voice. It was my lady standing quietly watching by the front door. "We'll go upstairs and I will show you your room."

My room? It was a tiny chamber with a small, deep-set window and a bed.

"I want you to bend down so that nobody can see you through the window from the houses in front," she said.

I sat on the bed and a tiny spark of a suspicion fired up in my head. I looked closely at her again, at the minimally powdered, serious face, her precision and poise. I could pick up no message.

"Now we will go down to the back of the house. So you can see his line of approach."

At the back of the house, there was a small garden and a wall about four feet high, which dropped about six feet into a field. The field was open, without trees. No one could approach unseen in daylight. At night, there would be no chance of climbing in over the wall with that dog on guard.

"Sometimes I hear him running across the roof."

I looked up at the tiles. Many were green with moss, slippery. The angle was too steep to climb even if they were dry. In any case, they would not stand the weight of an intruder. I turned back to her, deadpan.

"He runs across the roof?"

"Yes. I hear him."

She was looking straight into my eyes. Again, I had a flicker of suspicion at the back of my brain. I looked around again at the house. There was a back door into the kitchen in which the monster dog slept, on its left, four lattice windows in a row three feet high, only one of which opened. If it was closed, it looked as though an intruder would have to cut or batter his way through. He would make a racket, almost as loud as the howling warning from the dog.

We went inside to the living room and inspected the latch on the one window which could be opened. No way to reach it without breaking the glass. I went to the corner of the room on the other side of the fireplace from the window which opened and told her it would be my look-out for the night. I asked her for the sock, filled it with sand, and then held it under the tap in the kitchen until it was soaked.

"Is that your, the… er?"

"He can't get in unless someone opens the street door. The kitchen door is out of the question because of the dog. If he has some magic way of opening that window what comes in first is his head. That's what the sandbag is for. No blood, no noise."

She paused a moment. "You'll be awake all night. You must get some sleep. If you get in bed I will bring your supper."

When she came up to 'my room' she knelt on the side of the bed with her shiny, stockinged knees indenting the mattress, leaned in close and put the tray on my lap. She straightened up and, expressionless, looked for a split second into my eyes.

She went downstairs. I lay motionless, cursing myself. All you had to say very gently was, 'No one can get in here. No one can cross the roof. There is no intruder. There is something else. Just trust me. I will help you in any way I can. Just sit down here and tell me'. Of course, it would not have been easy coming from a youth of twenty-eight to a poised woman of forty or more, especially as I looked nothing like what I imagine was her vision of a Commando officer.

After dark I rehearsed my route in the living room past the fireplace to the window with my sock at shoulder height and then settled in the corner on the bare floorboards because I had no intention of even momentarily dozing.

The next moment, I opened my eyes. It was early daylight. Silhouetted against the windows was my lady in a long nightgown and bearing a breakfast tray. She put it on the table. And stared down at me, still prone.

"I had faith in you. I expected you to protect me, my son and household. And I find you not only asleep but snoring."

She left the room head held high. In searing shame I rolled into the foetal position gritting my teeth and screwing up my face into a gargoyle rictus. I jumped up, kicked the sock aside, and wrenched open a fast-stuck door in the corner. It led into a passage with, thank you God, a street door at the end of it. There were boxes, trunks, tall stacks of books, a bicycle, a pogo stick, a hat stand, and dusty lampshades in my way. I stumbled over the lot and tore at the door latch and lock. It opened a few inches among the clutter, enough for me to squeeze out. I crossed the street cringing about how this would look to the neighbours. My footsteps echoed on the silent, dawn-lit pavement, the only sound in the universe. But then a voice like a bell, filled with anguish, pealed among the cottages.

"Come back, Mr. Nott. Please don't go. Mr. Nott, come back."

I bent my head, did not look round and hurried on to the station, and the train, and London. Now, more than half a century later I close my eyes in the wakeful early hours and hear that pain-filled voice echoing down the street and down the years to twist my guts with remorse and self-contempt.

Chapter 21

Magic

Angel Falls, Sarisariñama, El Autana, magic words, magic places, and magic life events if you can get there. And if you can get all three? I had the good luck to do just that.

The Auyan-Tepui, 'Devil Mountain', because of its ferocious storms, is an 8,200-feet plateau in the Guyana jungles, southeast Venezuela, a remote region sparsely inhabited by Indian tribes. Some five hundred miles from the capital, Caracas, it is still largely unexplored. But its enthralling wonder is a gorge that cuts into it from the north where the highest falls on the planet, 3,380 feet, plunge down in one swoop three times higher than the Empire State. That the Devil Mountain's prize gem is called Angel is because that was the name of an adventuring US bush pilot who saw it flying through cloud in 1923.

The Pittsburgh Explorers' Club had twice attempted to make the first ascent of the wall of the falls. A climber on both tries, John Timo, twenty-eight, now mounted a third attack and asked me to join his team. They arrived in Caracas in a tiny *Mooney* single engine, owned and piloted by senior surgeon Paul Straub, thirty-eight, a strapping athlete in top condition with a surprisingly gentle manner. Third was George Bogel, twenty-six, big, gung-ho, new to wet, slime-streaked jungle climbing, who was later killed by an ice-fall in the Himalayas.

We flew 350 miles to Ciudad Bolivar on the Orinoco, one hundred and seventy-five more to an unlit, no-radio, grass airstrip and a further hundred and seventy-five miles to Camarata mission to which there are no roads. From here we would reach base camp after sixty miles in a dug-out canoe on four rivers: Acanan, Carrao, Churun and Angel, piloted by Camarateco Indian Gabriel and his crew. Here we sorted 300lbs. of gear into packs. Our rations were dehydrated powders. These needed water. The irony was that on this rain-swept 3,000-foot route, with daily tropical electric storms and flashing lightning all around us, we had to haul two 5-gallon tanks of water because the first attempt was forced down when the rain stopped for four days.

We followed the Angel River upwards, crossed it to go to the right of the falls, cut up between the base of the rock and the jungle to a fissure that promised a good start, and bivouacked for the night. We were on a steep little pinnacle with no ledges. We kept our boots on. Just one dropping off into space was the last thing we could afford to lose. We didn't take them off again for eleven days.

On the first day Paul fell, dragging me, who was above holding his rope, off my perch head-down holding him until he got back on the rock. Timo, sixty feet above with Bogel, swarmed down to help. It was the first and last time Straub needed a hand.

We spent the night on a ledge in hard rain, with no food and no sleeping gear. They were long hours to dawn. Our next day was hardly a tribute to team skill; Bogel was way up above on an overhang. I was forty feet below perched on a toe-hold waiting to follow. There was a sudden hullabaloo below. The water-pack had fallen along with Paul's climbing pack including his contact lens case, all clothing and sleeping bag. Timo, swinging round on the rope, found the water-pack miraculously hung up on a rock spike, and dragged it up to my stance, losing his anorak, where we fixed it to the rope up to Bogel. It was now dark. Night climbing is madness. Timo brought up Paul. I followed the fixed rope up to Bogel and eventually we were all above the overhang. We counted up. We had lost the bivouac lantern, most of the climbing gear – pitons, slings, étriers.

The doctor who had nothing but his pants and tee shirt, said, coolly, "I can travel faster without baggage. Even my pockets are empty."

We were now soaked, cold and covered in sap-slime and mud from pulling through ledges of bromeliads. We were surviving on one meal a day where we filled a pan with a sprinkle from now unreadable packs, stirred in water and passed it round taking three spoonfuls each until it was empty. It's called a hoosh by Brit climbers, I had preached at base camp. No plates or cups. You make your tea in the same pot when it's empty and that's it, no washing up.

"I'm interested in a fit team to reach the top, not cholera," Timo had said. Cholera or no we were a bit creaky on the seventh day when we reached the crux of the climb where Timo had been stopped by lack of a bong, a long V-shaped iron that would jam in a crack too wide for a piton. We watched him climb fifty near vertical feet. We listened to the bong being hammered in with a rising ping, saw him pull up, stand on it and reach the first handhold in eight smooth feet. We cheered. He had passed the 1969 high point. Eighty feet further up he belayed and Bogel followed. Straub went next. Me, now, because of my smart barrel hitch, the pack dispatcher, wrestled the wet rope round each slimy bag, clipped it on the haul rope while up top they heaved. There was a delay, then, a hundred and thirty feet above, I saw Timo traversing forty feet left across a smooth wall. He was in trouble. His legs started to tremble. He was on fingernail holds.

"Get back, John," I shouted, but he suddenly leaped forward in the air to land in a steep grassy gully, scrabbled and fought thirty feet up it to a stance. When I got up to Bogel it was dark. Night climbing again. He was on a wobbly stance, belay rope over a sharp-edged rock.

I was running my doubting hands over it when he put

my hand on a rope and said, "This is fixed, clip on to it and drop off the edge. John and Paul will pull you across with your waist rope."

A sudden wind thinned the cloud, and moonlight flashed down the wall lighting up the crinkled jungle 2,600 feet below. Few climbs have exposure like this. I glanced back at George, his face strained, wet with rain, and jumped. I dropped six feet, felt the alarming stretch of nylon rope and was heaved across like a boneless duffel bag. Once across I scrabbled up to Timo, slapping his back in applause. We looked down to see Bogel who fell at a right angle to the wall and sprinted across horizontally, a stunt we cheered. It's called a Tyrolean traverse and George knew how to do it. That night we could stretch out where the angle of the gully eased off.

Next morning we lugged the gear up easier ground to a flat space. Rising beyond it was two hundred feet of difficult rock. But we knew we'd hit what we'd feared most. We were on a pinnacle detached from the main face. We moved to the edge and looked down an immense chasm twelve feet wide, and hundreds of feet deep. The real top was up that vertical wall beyond it. We were stock still for a moment, not believing it, and then spread out along the edge. Nothing. Then there was a shout from Timo.

"There's a chockstone!"

We ran to him. It was fifteen feet below us, twenty-five feet long, twelve wide, and forty deep; a monster, but a mere pebble jammed in this thousand-foot cleft. Bogel went first, down, across, up thirty feet to a possible line leading to the left but with no belay.

I crossed to Bogel, passed him carefully because he was not tied on, went along the traverse and at twenty feet found a stance. Timo and Straub meanwhile brought the packs up from the bivouac, across to Bogel who then brought each one to me and returned for the next, very cool over a momentous drop with no security. At night in a wet alcove, grey-faced with exhaustion, we decided to eat what was left of our dehydrated food and water, and to make a dash for the summit and then a non–stop maybe two-day descent of the whole wall by rappel.

The final wall was more a line of towers cut apart by rain over millions of years. The falls shoot out from them two hundred feet below the summit. In front of us it was split by a narrow cleft two feet wide and sixty high. We followed this until it opened out into a moon crater cradling a crumbling ruin of stone. There were pinnacles, corners, cracks, walls and overhangs, the floor no more than jammed boulders beneath which were hundreds of feet of space. In nook and cranny grew plants fit for a madman's window-box, roots creeping up their stems, two feet wide and clinging to a half inch of dirt in a wrinkle of rock. They had been flourishing for millions of years before the oceans had swept over the land below and wiped out all life, surviving through millions more to feel at last the wondering touch of the first humans to see them.

Here the dinosaurs were millions of years in the future

and we four bedraggled intruders were eons out of our time. But right there the fanciful stopped. There was a forty-foot wall in front of us. From the top it sloped steeply and wet to a wide gap and continued upwards on the other side. Timo with coils of rope loosely in his hand ran down, leaped across and scrabbled up to a stance. I was next with a rope to him and one behind to Bogel. I slithered down the rock and fell into the gap. It was hundreds of feet deep and I had a bang on the head. Bogel slacked his rope and I swung to the far side, climbed out and crept up dizzily to Timo.

"Okay?" he said absently, already readying for Bogel's turn.

There was a second wall. Straub braced against the rock, Timo got onto his shoulders and then onto his upstretched arm. From there after a struggle with some wet holds he was soon on the ledge. I followed. While they heaved Bogel up I moved cautiously up a gully of greasy boulders. There was open sky above and a feel of open air; six more feet of rock and a scraggly plant.

Timo camo up to me. I said, "You go first, John, it's your route."

He climbed out, looked round and leaned down to us. "Gentlemen, this is the top," he said. We joined him and stared around; nobody in the whole world knew where we were and all we could see was mist.

A quick photo, a note of the climb under a rock and we dropped without a word into the gully, down the walls, across the gap, down again, and snatched up what was left in the alcove. We continued down amidst a tremendous storm of rain, wind and lightning. Level with us, even below us, the thunder was booming without a break. At the Tyrolean we forgot a rope, shrugged and went on as fast as we could rappel. Dark caught us on a steeply sloping ledge running with muddy water, cascading over the edge into unknown depths. This was a long night slithering down to the edge if we dozed or sitting up shivering. At first light we moved, wet, hungry, cold, and sleepless, what else? The storm stopped at midday. Five hours more and we landed on flat ground. We scrabbled around looking for tinder and dry branches. We had a smoke bomb we were to ignite when a TV plane approached. We never saw it. Now we crouched round a small pile of damp foliage, shivering. We detonated the bomb and shoved it in blowing as hard as we could. There was a faint flicker but there was a faint familiar patter too: rain. It burst on us again so we lay there under a sleeping bag zippered open and wet through in three minutes.

A few hours after dawn we reached base on the river Acanan. Empty.

'Had to go back. No food', was scrawled in charcoal on a cardboard box. But no date.

We had thought about floating along four rivers sixty miles to Camarata with no food. But for the moment we ripped open the box. Spaghetti.

We made a fire and put a handful in the water, but

Straub shouted, "Put it all in. What the hell?" He jumped up, yelling, "We're starving!"

Shocked, we leaped up to restrain him but he laughed and pointed behind us. There, round the bend came a long, grey curiara, the skipper's grin splitting his mahogany face. It was Gabriel and his Indians.

Heavy backpack trouble on El Autana, Venezuela, 1972

Jungle breakfast in the Amazonas

On top of Angels Four, after ten day climb 1971

Sarisarinama, Venezuela, 1974, new style climbing outfit,
mechanics overalls, different colour for each man

Soaked author rappels down to caves from ledge on west face of El Autana

Steve Platt leads hard pitch on North Ridge, El Autana, before being washed off by storm.

Where jungle meets rock. Looking for a route on El Autana, Venezuela, 150kms from nearest road, 1973

Chapter 22

Epilogue

From illegitimate birth in a Liverpool workhouse for destitute women, my pregnant mother having been thrown out by her parents who were preparing to take ship to winter yet again in sunny Gibraltar, to a commission in the Kings Own Yorkshire Light Infantry, a trooper in 21st SAS, Cambridge, Fleet Street, and finally in 1960, recruitment into MI6 at a 'luncheon' in White's, a lordly London club. Right at a hot moment in the Cold War.

This was made to measure. I never saw an office, never had a boss looking over my shoulder, never had a glint-eyed colleague salivating for me to blunder, and never had to endure the slow corporate ladder. Many, many wild nights; who the hell cared?

I worked entirely alone, with no emergency contact with my case officer (or my family), often a thousand miles away, for thirty years. A particular task was to infiltrate any rebel, leftish, discontented anti-government group to pick out any Soviet-influenced, mainly Cuban, troublemaker who had himself infiltrated, or founded. What to do in any situation was up to me.

I worked in nineteen countries, many no more than small islands. These were smiling, sunny and very difficult. I'd catch the early morning island-hopping flight in Trinidad and was often the only passenger to get off the plane and walk to the wood-cabin airport office and its crowd of curious idlers.

"Hey, you dat pressman was here last month looking for a hurricane?" It soon got to the groups. "What d'hell he want now?" I'd go into a routine.

"Hot, man. Cold beer? Let's get a crate. The newspaper will pay bless 'em."

Later, a courtesy call to the premier's office shaking hands with everyone and a news question, "How's it going with the Caribbean Federation?" Nowhere, as if we all didn't know.

The Firm let me get away on seven expeditions in the Amazonas of Venezuela, a first ascent of the face of Angel Falls, the first penetration of El Autana Caves and the Sarisariñama Sinkhole, and discovering new routes in the Andes with George's band of the 1953 Everest team. They quite approved when my books *Angels Four* and *Descent To The Lost World,* appeared because spooks don't get up to these goings-on. It was great cover. In fact they approved so much that they lent me the money to buy a thirty-foot sailboat to cross the Atlantic to help recover from being divorced by my most beautiful wife Mariela who rightly, after twelve years of absences and mucho rum-coke, wanted out, in 1977.Naturally, the condition was that as soon as I landed I'd start working again.

Of course, there were moments when I thought I was in the movies like when a Guatemalan secret police goon pushed me against the wall, his gun in my ribs and said, "Get in the car or I'll kill you," or when three Jamaican 'revolutionaries' got me in a quarry and threatened, "We goin' kill you, white boy." There were many more. I had assets here. I'm five foot seven near enough, 140lbs, with a face like a padre. In espionage theory, I was inconspicuous. Friends from rumbustious nights in grog shops earlier in life said I got away with hell-knows what because I don't look dangerous, and posed no threat.

By 1987 after years of no-cover they sent me to a doctor in the City of London, top stress zone. He pronounced me burned out.

"There's no cure. Whatever you're doing, stop it."

No way. They gave me funds for a fortnight in Spain to get over it. Fidgety, I left after a week and went back to the dirty wars in Guatemala and El Salvador. Four more years. At one point my case officer airily suggested I take my third wife Tomi and small daughter Carina, to San Salvador, and settle them in a star hotel while I foraged around. Like spooks don't have families with them? However you look at it, MI6 is a grand unit.

I'm eighty-nine now, a bit bored and can't handle high-tech communications but even now if they asked me in their inimitable way, "Do you think you could take a look around in Syria?" I'd go.

About the Author

Born
Liverpool UK, 11.10.28

Army
Commissioned Duke of Cornwall's Light Infantry.
Served in Somaliland 1947-1949
Joined 21st SAS 1952

University
Cambridge, St Catharine's College, 1949-52. BA
Mod Lang (French, Spanish), and Law
University of Wales, Aberystwyth, Postgrad
Diploma in Education, 1954

Jobs
Instructor Outward Bound Mountain School,
Eskdale, 1954

Liverpool Daily Post to 1957, then Reuters, launched Geneva Weekly Tribune, then Daily Mirror news sub 1959. From 1960 free lance in Venezuela and the Caribbean, then in Nicaragua, El Salvador, Guatemala 1981-1991.

Treks

Seven expeditions in the Amazonas, south Venezuela. Member of the first team to climb the wall of Angels Falls, ten days and nights on the face. First to enter the Autana caves. First down the 1000-foot Sarisariñama sink hole. Four new routes in the Andes with George Band of the Everest team.. Took NBC and Nippon-TV teams on repeats of Autana and Sarisariñama to make documentaries of these explorations.

Atlantic

Sailed 31-foot sloop from Plymouth, UK, to Jamaica. 1978. Then through the Canal and up to San Diego, CA, 1980